Topsham Lock, the Lower Sluice & the Back Gut

Fragments concerning
The Port of Topsham River Commissioners (1840–2023) as
established under the Exeter Port Dues Act 1840, whilst touching
Upon Matters relating to the River Exe & Estuary (1539–1850),
and the Construction of Topsham Lock, following the Law Suit of
Robert Davy & others v. the Exeter Chamber (1828–1829)

Tom Epton

Published by Tom Epton
All rights reserved

This book is sold subject to the condition that it shall not, by way of trade or otherwise, be lent, resold, hired out, or otherwise circulated without the publisher's prior consent in any form of binding or cover other than that in which it is published and without a similar condition including this condition being imposed on the subsequent publisher.

Copyright © Tom Epton, 2023. The moral right of the author has been asserted.

Tom Epton, Topsham, Exeter EX3 0AE
First published in the United Kingdom, 2023

ISBN 978-1-3999-5150-0

Edited by Mike Patrick of Black Oar Publications
Design and Typeset by Ned Hoste of The Big Ideas Collective
Printed by Mixam, Watford, UK

Illustration on front cover:
Topsham Lock - view towards Topsham across the River Exe
Aerial photos on p34 thanks to Topsham Museum
Other aerial shots on the cover and in the book taken by Jo Stephens

Typeset in Adobe Garamond and Garamond Premier

Dedication

to the Ancient Mariner **James Delmar Norton ("Jim")** *of Topsham for his Friendship and in Recognition and Celebration of his 42 Years of unbroken Service as an Elected Port of Topsham River Commissioner and as a former Commodore of Topsham Sailing Club and former Chairman of Topsham Small Craft Club.*

Acknowledgements with Thanks

Jim Norton

Mr Grahame Forshaw, MBE, MNI, Harbourmaster for the Port of Exeter

Bill Ricketts – Topsham Sailing Club, Yard Marshal & former Commodore

Peter Williams – Topsham Sailing Club, a former Commodore; the Master & Great Helmsman of "*Capella*" of Topsham

Allen & Rosey Heavens – Topsham Sailing Club and the Topsham Lock Cottage, where Rosey was born and spent her childhood and youth

Alan Caig – former Director of Leisure & Museums, Exeter City Council – a pillar of Estuary Players, Topsham & the playwright of "*The First Cut - or Isabella's Revenge*"

Dr Penny Bayer – Topsham Local Historian

Nancy Epton

Phil Bonser – Friendly Computer Man & Clarinettist

The Institution of Civil Engineers, London (Carol Morgan)

Ashfords, Solicitors, Exeter (Lara Moore & her Ports Team)

Topsham Museum (Catriona Batty, Gill McLean and Mike Patrick)

The Devon Heritage Centre, Exeter

The Harbour Board for the Port Authority of the City of Exeter

Exeter City Council (Waterways)

The Port of Topsham River Commissioners (1840 to 2023)

Topsham Sailing Club (*established 1885*)

Topsham Lock c 1840 by E.H.Hurdle. Courtesy of a private collection

Topsham Lock

Proud but forlorn now stands Topsham Lock.
At ease in silent Dignity, the quiet Observer of Ebb and Flow,
Strong its Buttresses in Power and Purpose, tide-water held
as if 'twixt Two Vast and Trunkless Legs of Giant,
Abandoned by Man to slow Decay,
Victim to the Ravages of uncivilised Times.
Here, Mud-moored anchored, these Honourable Slabs,
their History-Memories taped in Stone,
The Software of Lived Experience data-stored within,
Awaiting some future Download and Text Transcription
by Those to come hereafter with Technik beyond our ken.
Fashioned by King's Bench Suit in 1829 Court of Law,
Came forth the Topsham Hero, worthy Robert Davy
A Man of Countess Wear, Centenarian all bar 50 days,
He who supplied the Stone, from his own Quarries hewn,
Shipbuilder, Merchant, Trader – blind for 40 Years.

The Lock, now stanked-off from Canal and River both,
Bereft its Gates, Lock Cottage bleak and vacant,
Its Keepers so long gone, their lives Recorded in Ledgers, Lists
-inadequate Archives of our Pasts, played out on Muted Strings.
We now glide past, "Capella" silent on Evening Tide,
the Race fulfilled, all Canvas furled, the Day is done.

With what Voice and Song, I ask, might Topsham Lock now speak?
Can still be heard the Creak of Hinge, the Swing of Beam,
the swirl of Lock-gate Paddle, a splash of Warp or Line?
Why is there no longer Gossip, Keeper's Banter, words familiar?
Where now are Sailor Simmons and daughter Rosey,
the bleat of Keeper's Goat, the bustle of chickens cooped?
Who now Cranes up the Whitebait, to make "that bit extra"
 – a salary top-up to the £100 per annum, fixed since 1826?
I say again, with what Voice and Song might Topsham Lock now speak?
Small things all, but, in their importance, the Essence of the All, -
The very "stuff" of Life - and of our own Mortality.

Topsham Lock

Here no longer flow the waters of Exe through shuttered Pound,
But let not Topsham Lock sleep unhonoured –
Its ever patient and uplifting Presence deserves no Death.
Shall it now be left by Man in passive desolation?
Colossal Wreck,
Mud-bound, Gateless and bare,
as the deep and languid Estuary Sands stretch far away …

Tom Epton

Contents

The Acknowledgements		4
Introduction		10
The Maps		14
Abbreviations and Glossary		17
Chapter One	The Port of Topsham River Commissioners (TRCs) – their Provenance	18
Chapter Two	The Historical Context	25
Chapter Three	The Lower Sluice & the Back Gut	30
Chapter Four	James Green and his Two Reports of 1820 & 1824	35
Chapter Five	The Canal Extension Act 1829	43
Chapter Six	Robert Davy - Man of Topsham	50
Chapter Seven	The Court Case – Robert Davy & Others v. Exeter Chamber	55
Chapter Eight	The Agreement 26th March 1829: Robert Davy & Chamber	65
Chapter Nine	Hubris and Nemesis	73
Chapter Ten	The Commissioners' Report on Exeter and the Chamber 1834	83
Chapter Eleven	The Exeter Port Dues Act 1840	90
Chapter Twelve	The Interlink between (a) the Canal Extension Act 1829 & Topsham Lock and (b) the Exeter Port Dues Act 1840	96
Chapter Thirteen	The current Statutory Basis empowering the Port of Exeter	99
Chapter Fourteen	The Last Major Achievements of the TRCs in 2023	100
Chapter Fifteen	A Final Coda and Reflection including the Demise of the TRCs	102
Afterword		105

The Appendices

Appendix 1	The Historical Context (National).	109
Appendix 2	Exeter & Plymouth Gazette – Extracts from the Revd. George Oliver's essay on Early Navigation of the Exe &c. (1826).	112
Appendix 3	Extracts from the Minutes of the Proceedings of The Institution of Civil Engineers, Transactions Vol. IV, session 1845, with Abstracts of the Discussions and with John Green's Reports as a Continuation of the Memoir of the Canal of Exeter, from 1563 to 1724, by Philip Chilwell De la Garde, including the relevant Appendices (A) and (B) therewith.	116
Appendix 4	Extracts from the Canal Extension Act 1829 relating to Topsham Lock.	123
Appendix 5	Extracts from the Robert Davy Case v. The City of Exeter, under the Title of *The King v. The Mayor, Bailiffs and Commonalty of Exeter,* as reported at length under the Court's decision dated 11th February 1829.	127
Appendix 6	Extracts from the Public Speech of the Mayor, Robert Rogers Sanders, as reported by the Exeter and Plymouth Gazette on Saturday 2nd October 1830.	142
Appendix 7	Letters to the Western Times (various).	144
Appendix 8	The Commissioners' Report into Exeter 1834.	155

Introduction

All history is but a collection of fragments, such as found in the random and uncoordinated shards within a kaleidoscope, that hardware of daily life, but assembled and thrown together by each individual out of their own private memories, experiences, traumas, prejudices, education, fears, ancestry, books and films, culture, faith, family, whatever, wherever, before being distilled through the unique lens of their own individual and subjective "view of things".

We each forge, code and construct our own Identities and private Software, to install in our personal telescope through which we can observe the world, before mortality then shatters it, casting its pieces into the abyss, leading our successors to ignore or pick up and reassemble whatever fragments they might wish – or stumble upon. There are no absolutes: all things are relative. The Facts might well be sacred but a Truth might also be found in the Story. For each of us, we carry our own story, our own truth - even if with Gaps in between the lines. It is within such Gaps that the story within the story might be discovered – that private Voyage into the Known Unknowns….

This Book, with all its Gaps, represents some of the fragments that have been carried into my own days here in the Town of Topsham, forming a key part of a life in which simply being out on the Waters of the Exe has become its own inspired River of Being, reflecting the multitude of hours spent under sail.

It has been my position as Clerk to the Port of Topsham River Commissioners, established by statute under the Exeter Port Dues Act 1840, that first prompted the structure of this book, allied to the timing by the Estuary Players of Topsham's fine stage production in 2018 of "*The First Cut - or Isabella's Revenge*" (see page 160) - a panoramic history of the construction of Exeter Canal, written by Alan Caig, the former director of Leisure & Museum Services at Exeter City Council, who generously gave me access to his own historical research papers. In addition, once my "Argument" had been conceived, then I could not have developed it without the academic support, encouragement and friendship of Michael Patrick, who, as an established local historian and publisher, has given so much of his time and technical skills without stint, to provide the host of research leads required, as well as challenging those aspects which needed good evidence. In addition, hours spent at the welcoming Devon Heritage Centre are never wasted.

Always have I understood that volumes and decades of valuable research and study have already been carried out by academic historians upon near parallel aspects of my own amateur contribution, to which works I have strived to give full acknowledgement and respect. If I have failed to do so in any instance, then I hasten to apologise. My concern has been to till the soil and tend the grapes within the modesty of our River Commissioners' vineyard, rather than tread on the growths in the grander vineyards of professional colleagues.

Allied with a pervading and ever-increasing curiosity about Humanity and the World in general, where we are but temporary Visitors, it is because of my own long life in the Law and its Practice, with a sustained interest in its legal history, that I found a Vine that had not been nurtured previously within the *domaine* of any other Vigneron.

The serendipity of this opening was a gift, which my introduction to the Port of Topsham River Commissioners has helped foster, as well also in my being supported within the Hallowed Gates of Topsham Sailing Club. I had been provided with the kernel of a modest original research project, one that is the sole justification for this book. The conjunction in timings is fortuitous by reason both of personal old age and also the imminent demise of the River Commissioners, whose world I wished to catch before they fade away after Sunset over the Haldon Hills and vanish into the gathering crepuscular twilight.

At this point please be aware that my Argument is centred on "the James Green Swerve" between his two Canal Improvement Reports, of 1820 and 1824. These were followed by Robert Davy's Court Case against the City of Exeter in 1828/9 and then by his Agreement, which was reached with the Chamber on the 26th March 1829. What must be seen as the Mercantile backcloth which precipitated the whole matter were the two problems arising, first with the technical inadequacies of the Lower Sluice and, secondly, with the Tide-channel (Back Gut), the latter as an artificial Channel cut in order to create a navigable channel for the improved passage of Cargoes between the existing and historic Topsham Channel (the upriver end of which ran very close to the Western Bank of the River at the point where Topsham Lock later came to be constructed in 1832) and the Lower Sluice, which was the Entrance to the Lighter Canal, as it sought to become a larger Ship Canal, to cater for increasing cargo traffic in larger vessels.

I have been obliged to make contextual references of the Canal's Extension to Turf Pool as well as to historical matters generally but I have no arguments to raise against the actual Canal Extension to Turf and Turf Lock, per se, save as to the circumstances and consequences of the financial disaster that their construction works had created and also, as a small cloud on the far horizon, concern about the future effects of Climate Change affecting the Estuary generally and the vulnerabilities of the massive embanked earthworks required to uphold this extended Section of the Canal in particular.

The Histories of the Exeter Canal and the Exe Estuary and River as well as of the City of Exeter have been so well covered, recorded and archived by so many professional individuals and bodies, upon whose shoulders I fear to tread, I can but only emphasise that my sole purpose has been to espy Topsham Lock as my "special subject" and find a chink in the Tapestry of Topsham's own History. As a certain Leonard Cohen says "There is a crack in everything, that's how the light gets in".

The one "Golden Nugget" discovered, by bizarre chance or mis-happence, in the Devon Heritage Centre (DHC) Archives was the original Agreement dated 26th March 1829 between Robert Davy and the Exeter Chamber for the construction of Topsham Lock, which had proved the key to the parties avoiding the otherwise lengthy and expensive further Court proceedings in the King's Bench, by way of a Writ of Indictment at Common Law, even if to be based on the same arguments as presented and pleaded on the 11th February 1829 under the Rule for the Prerogative Writ of Mandamus. This Rule was obtained in May 1828 by Sir James Scarlett KC. It was issued in the name of the King on behalf of the 5 Topsham Traders, of whom Robert Davy was the principal instigator– and funder - of the Suit. My considered view is that Robert Davy stands worthy of being properly called "the Hero of Topsham" – a Man without whose leadership the dignity and commercial prosperity of the Town would have been compromised and put in peril.

As I am not native to Topsham, and thus now engaged with the Town as an "Outsider", if it were to be asked by what right or qualification I might speak of Topsham affairs, then I cannot but invoke the words of that mystic and Prophet, Kahlil Gibran, to the effect that: "It is better to view the Mountain when standing on the Plain".

I also would pray in aid the value of Oral History, as encouraged by my late friend, Mr George Ewart Evans, whose pioneering work was to listen to and record (by use of primitive recording devices and not by way of an equally valid but more imaginative or poetic recall) the Voices and Stories of the Old Ways in the lives of elderly local people, whose language and dialects were at risk of being forgotten and unheard, as modern ways changed everything, apart from the devastation of local cultures caused by two World Wars. Hence, one now appreciates the valuable work achieved by Topsham Museum in preserving, by its fine archive, many of the Voices of the Unheard of Topsham and its historic Port. In addition, Words, even if fragments, can still keep the flame of an historical "conversation" alight, as many an hour spent at Topsham Sailing Club has been gifted to me over past decades - words without agenda or purpose but enabling a fund of Tales of Estuary Life to be recaptured and re-told, with all their undertones of petty triumphs won and disasters survived. Yes, the Facts are always vital but Truth also lurks within the Story. It is by such stories and memories that our Identities are established and maintained. They are the Software links for our individual kaleidoscopes – some of our Fragments....

Once the proposed Harbour Revision Order is enacted under the Harbours Act 1964, (as amended) then the role of the Port of Topsham River Commissioners will be subsumed within the powers and authority of the Harbour Board, as the governing body for the Port Authority of Exeter. We will cease to exist, our corporate kaleidoscope shattered....

Tom Epton - Topsham - 21st February 2023

"Cast a Cold Eye
On Life, on Death,
Yachtman, Sail by..."

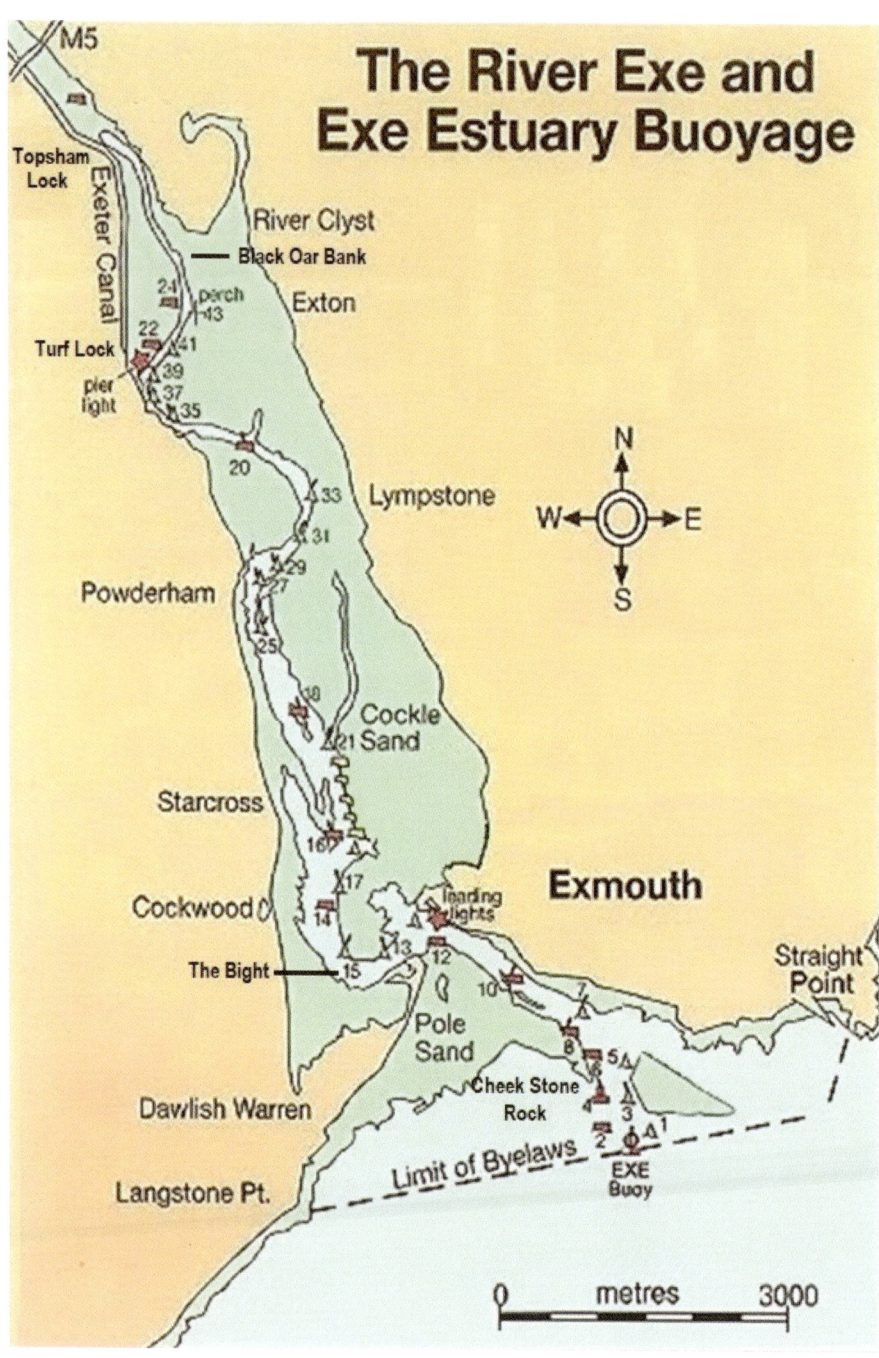

Exe estuary

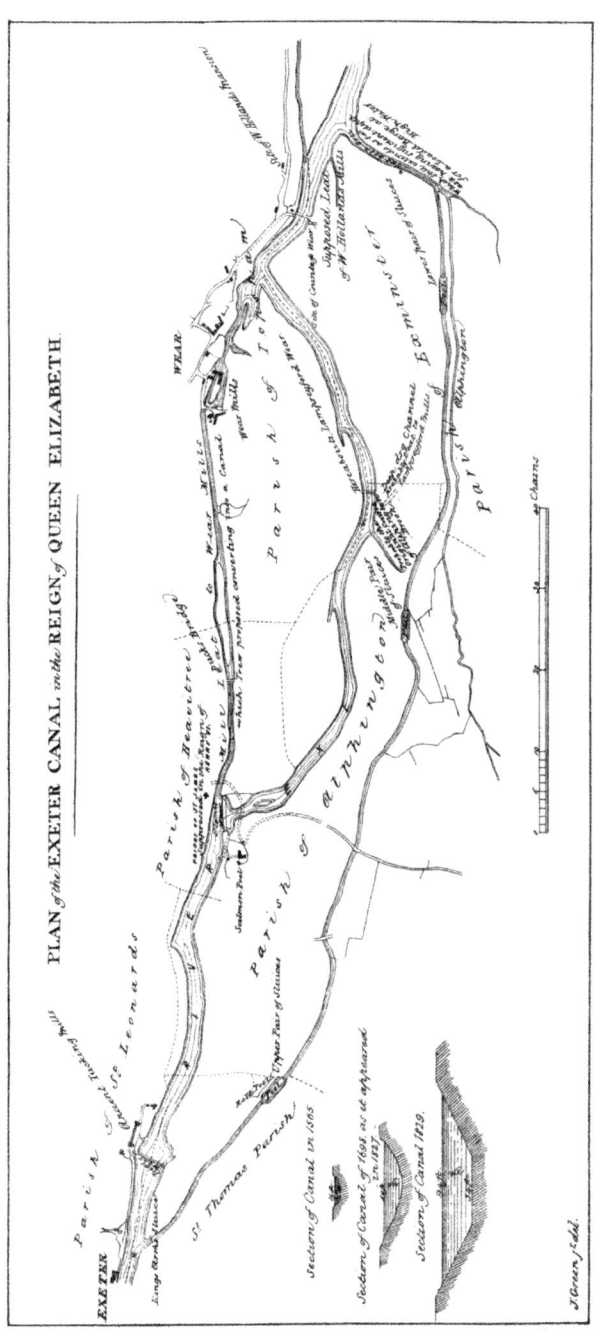

Plan of Exeter Canal in the Reign of Queen Elizabeth I (drawn by James Green)

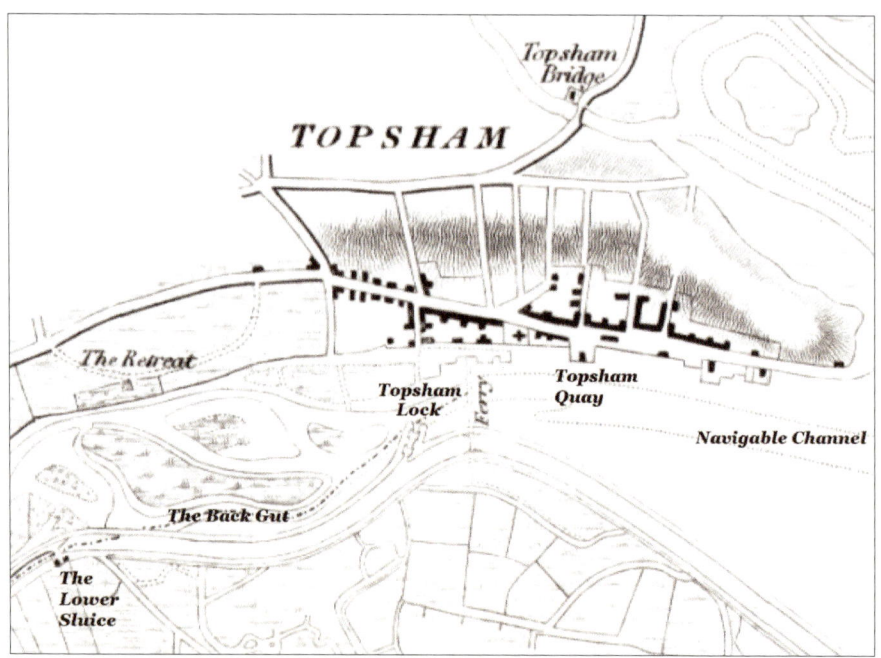

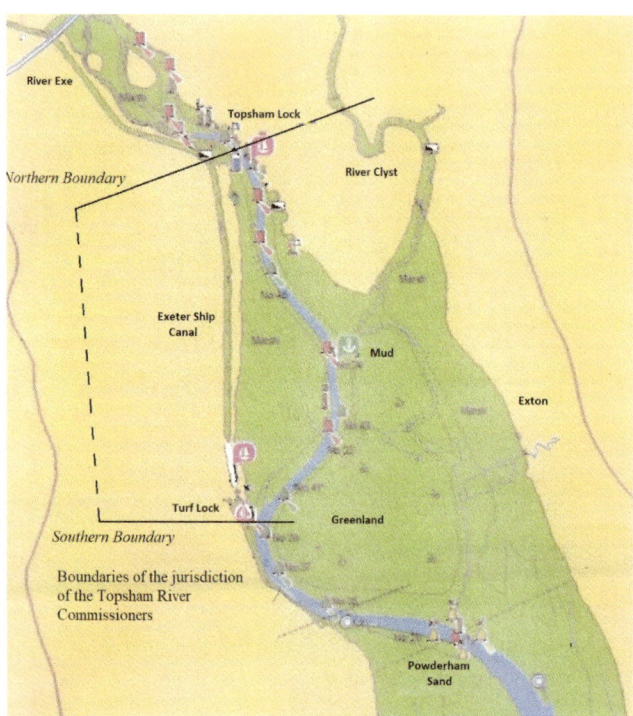

Top: James Green's plan c.1828
Below: Boundaries of the jurisdiction of the Topsham River Commissioners

Abbreviations and Glossary

TRCs - The Port of Topsham River Commissioners.

HB - The Harbour Board for the statutory Port of Exeter.

HRO - Harbour Revision Order (under the Harbours Act 1964).

ECC - Exeter City Council (under whose aegis the HB functions).

NC - The Navigation Committee of the Chamber (established in 1814).

The Chamber - The Governing body of Exeter for 700 years until 1835.

Tides - Tides in the sea are produced by a varying gravitational field associated with the relative orbits of the sun, earth and moon. In combination with the rotation of the earth this ensures that most of the sea areas on the globe are subject to daily changes of the depth of the sea. The majority of seaside locations experience two high tides and two low tides each day on a cyclic basis. The effect of the monthly lunar cycle progressively changes the relative alignment of the sun and moon so that tidal heights vary, again cyclically, with two extra-high (**Spring**) tides each month and two extra- low (**Neap**) tides each month.

Tidal Range - The difference between daily High Water (HW) & Low Water (LW) levels.

High Tides & Low Tides – occur twice every day but apply most importantly in conditions of "Spring" and "Neap" Tides.

Springs - Spring Tides occur when the Moon & the Sun are in alignment (when the Tidal Range is greatest).

Neaps - Neap Tides occur when the Moon & Sun are minimally aligned (when the Tidal Range is lowest or "more modest").

Shoals - These are Banks of Mud and/or Gravel accumulated by weather conditions, seasonal patterns and River-born sediment deposition in parts of the navigable Channel. They may restrict the passage of Vessels at Lower Tidal levels and form a key part of the story in this Book.

CHAPTER ONE

The Port of Topsham River Commissioners - Their Provenance

The Port of Topsham River Commissioners ("the TRCs") were established as a statutory corporate body in **1840** *(3 Victoria Sess.1840)* under the private Act of Parliament entitled the **Exeter Port Dues Act** ("the 1840 Act") for two Main Purposes being:-

> **A).** For *"equalising, defining and regulating the Petty Customs, and for facilitating the Collection thereof, and of the Quay Dues payable to the Mayor, Aldermen and Burgesses of the City and Borough of Exeter"* in their legal capacity as the statutory owners of the Port ("the Statutory Harbour Authority").

For such statutory purposes, the Port was defined by the 1840 Act in terms of its geographical boundaries, namely as being such parts of the River Exe and its Estuary as flow up to its entrance into the Sea *"at a place or rock called the Cheek Stone Rock"*. (This definition of "the Port of Exeter" is in use for all continuing practical purposes after the 1840 Act, which includes all the individual Ports and Quays in the Estuary but with the Topsham Quay and the City of Exeter Quay declared as the two principal trading Quays within the Port). Despite the above definition, the Port of Topsham is still so defined, in its own discrete legal entity, as a duly designated and registered "Fisheries Port" (*Sea Fish Industry Act 1951)*. In addition, its usage and historic description as the "Port of Topsham" is still recognised from past times as a discrete Port when it was, for all usage and general purposes, the principal trading Port of the City of Exeter, because of its deep water access and navigable channel, advantages denied to the City. Hence the need for the substantive Lighter and Barge traffic upriver from Topsham, both before and after the first Canal which was cut in 1563/4, in order to create a waterway link between the Quays of Topsham and Exeter, as an alternative to the packhorse and cartage transport required for portage over the inadequate roadways and tracks which hither thereto had benefitted from a *de facto* monopoly of the carriage of Goods with their accompanying charging rates.

Until the 1840 Act, there had been payable to the Port of Exeter "the said petty customs, duties or sums of money called "the Town Dues" which were payable under a much wider historical definition of the Port of Exeter, as one stretching from Axmouth to the East and to Teignmouth in the West. The limits of this wide definition of the Port were described in the Royal Commission of 1688 *(under William 3rd)* as being *"from the southernmost point of land on the East side of the mouth of the River Ex…in a supposed right line of the southernmost point of land on the West side of the Haven of Tingmouth with all the channels, roads, stream river base havens and crooks unto the quay commonly called the quay of Exon"*.

The 1840 Act expressly omitted these further *"creeks, harbours, place or places"* beyond the Cheek Stone Rock from its provisions so that their liabilities to pay Town Dues would continue to be charged as before.

As a by-note, those "retained" Town Dues are now no longer raised or collected by the City, having fallen by the wayside, despite certain Court Cases in the 19th Century, which had challenged their liability to be paid. The Cases remain of great interest to the legal scholar and historian and for completeness of reference, two such Cases are accessible for reading in the local Press Reports:-

(i) *The Mayor & Corporation of Exeter v. Warren (1844)5QB 773 Lord Denman*

(ii) *Mayor, Aldermen & Burgesses of Exeter v. Lawrence- Court of Exchequer - 31st January 1872 Lord Chief Baron and Baron Cleasby, (sitting in Banco).*

With the 1840 Act having abolished the Town Dues for the Port of Exeter, in lieu thereof they were replaced by *"the several tolls, duties and sums of money set forth in the Schedule to this Act annexed ("Quay Dues")* with powers for the Port of Exeter to raise and increase, alter, modify and regulate the various rates etc. The Schedule to the 1840 Act constitutes some five pages, listing all the items in alphabetical order, from Alum to Yarn Wick. e.g. Feathers are 2d per cwt, Bacon 1d per cwt, a Chariot or chaise 3s.00d.

The 1840 Act contains a careful and precise reference to the right of the Port of Exeter to *"certain quay dues payable on certain goods landed at the quay of the city of **Exeter** and at the quay of the town of **Topsham**, in the County of Devon"*.

We can emphasise these two Quays, for reasons to be developed in the following Chapters relating to both the historical context, and also to the then commercial circumstances, because under clause 3 of the 1840 Act ("Rates to be charged equally") it is clear that:

"the several tolls, duties and sums of money set forth in the said Schedule shall be at all times charged equally to all persons and after the same rate in respect of the several goods, wares and merchandizes, articles and things mentioned or referred to in the said Schedule, and no reduction or advance in any such charge shall be made, either directly or indirectly, in favour of or against any particular company or person".

This wording seeks to ensure that there was to be no favouritism or "special terms" or "cut rates" to be contemplated, such as might induce a trader to use either Topsham or Exeter Quay in preference to the other – such drafting and turn of phrase taking into account "human nature" in trading and commercial activities as well as concerns, controversy, apprehensions and "sensitivities" at that time…with special reference to former Tolls having been overtaken by the Exeter Chamber's wish to much increase their income by way of manifold increased tolls, in order to cover their losses and excesses, apart from dignity and loss of corporate "face" in having extended the Canal to Turf in such an improvident manner, which will be explored in the following Chapters.

This provision in the 1840 Act is set out in full because the "belt & braces" drafting makes manifest the attempt to bring an end, once and for all, to the mercantile rivalry that had subsisted between the two Quays, at Exeter and Topsham, for centuries and which had been brought to a head in 1828 by the Extension of the Ship Canal down to Turf Pool by the Exeter Chamber, with its ensuing and catastrophic effects upon the Chamber's corporate finances. It had also triggered a major Court Case brought by Robert Davy and 4 other Topsham merchants, to which later reference in detail will be made. One outcome came with the Canal Extension Act 1829, which gave some financial cover for the Chamber to cover their losses as well as some balm to the dignity of the Town of Topsham and the commercial prosperity and future prospects for Topsham Quay by providing for the construction of Topsham Lock (as a result of the Court Case).

B). For *"preserving the Navigation of the River Exe"*.

As at 2023, these provisions are the sole statutory amendments to the **River Exe Act 1539** which was an *Acte Publicke* Act of Parliament under the reign of Henry VIII *(Anno 31 Henrici, VIII, AD 1539)*.

[Other National legislation might well affect the Port such as the Marine Navigation Act 2013 or relating, say, to Merchant Shipping or the Environment, whilst this Book seeks to narrate the narrower canvas as related in its Title, namely Topsham Lock and its history in relation to the Extension of the Ship Canal from the Lower Sluice to Turf Pool].

Because of its importance, the provisions of the main terms of the River Exe Act 1539 are enshrined in the 1840 Act, which recites it as follows:-

> *"An Act for the mending of the Ryver of Exeter, the Mayor, Bailiffs and Commonalty of the city of Exeter, the predecessors of the said Mayor, Aldermen and Burgesses, and their successors, are empowered to pluck down, digg, moyne, breke, bank and cast up all and all matter of weyres, rocks, sands, gravel, and other letts and noysances whatsoever they be, in the river of Exe, and also in other places and grounde convenient and necessarie for the same whose soever they be, lying betweene the city of Exeter and the high*

sea, and further to do and make all other things requisite and necessarie, whereby shippes, boats and vessels may have their sure course and recourse in the said river to and from the said city, and there to charge and discharge their goods and merchandizes, without lett or disturbance of any person or persons; and it is expedient that the powers of the said Act be amended and enlarged".

So, between 1539 and 1840 there were no other statutory interventions of any kind in respect of the maintenance and the management of the Port of Exeter, save for the Canal Extension Act of 1829. It is to be noted that the construction of the first Lighter Canal in 1563 was a private venture of the Chamber of the City and was not empowered by or under any private Act of Parliament under the reign of Elizabeth 1st. This part of the history was recited in the pleadings of the Mandamus Court Case brought by Robert Davy in 1829.

Under Clause 15 of the 1840 Act, the new local Government authority that was created following the enactment of the Municipal Corporations Act 1835, which had abolished the Chamber (being the Mayor, Bailiffs and Commonalty of the City of Exeter) and had replaced it with a new corporate body (being the Mayor, Aldermen and Burgesses of the City and Borough of Exeter) (called "ECC" for the continuing purposes of this Book) was charged with using the funds collected from the Quay Dues to pay the Commissioners when appointed (as the 1840 Act later proceeded to do) sums for them to lay out and expend in each year, as required in any such year,

"in cleansing and keeping clear the channel leading to and round the public quay at Topsham belonging to the said Mayor, Aldermen and Burgesses, and the entrance to the lock above the town of Topsham, and in the deepening the channel of the River Exe, and in improving and preserving the navigation of the said river, from New Lane (now Ashford Road), in the parish of Topsham aforesaid, to the entrance of the creek leading to Turf Lock, in the parish of Exminster, in the County of Devon,….etc etc".

This Clause represents the definition of our "Jurisdiction" as TRCs in terms of maintaining the Navigation Channel for this part of the River. A copy of the Map of the River is enclosed as part of the Maps section preceding this Chapter One, showing the geographical extent of such Jurisdiction. The contextual purpose for such a specifically defined part of the River was to ensure an equality of navigation as between:

(i) that Section of River from Topsham Lock, which (under the Canal Extension Act 1829) in 1832 had replaced the site of the former Lower Sluice, higher up the River – (near the present M5 Motorway flyover bridge) leading downriver to the Turf Pool, as well as serving Topsham Quay, and

(ii) that Section of the Canal as had been extended in 1826 from the

Lower Sluice down to Turf, thereby by-passing Topsham Quay, which had resulted in the Canal Extension Act 1829 and which also had provided for the construction of Topsham Lock to appease the town of Topsham and preserve the commercial usage and trade at Topsham Quay (as a result of the Robert Davy Court Case).

(i.e. there were now two parallel Navigation Channels to maintain, the one being the Canal Extension, the other remaining the old and original "Topsham Channel").

The Minute Books of the TRCs from the 1840 Act onwards *(as held at DHC)* reveal the continuous works and expense involved in dredging and maintaining this vital Navigation Channel downriver from Topsham Lock. As at 2023, all drainage operations have effectively ceased with the lack of any commercial traffic on the River. However, let this liability not be overlooked. It was substantial. In the *"Queen Mab" Case - (Messrs. Lloyd as Owners of the ketch Queen Mab v. Exeter Town Council – His Hon. Judge Edge, Exeter County Court 8 & 9 July 1889 – Judgment 10 September 1889)*, evidence had been given by a Mr Holman, superintendent for dredging the River for the TRCs, that they *"took up between 2,000 and 3,000 tons of mud from here (i.e. the Quay) every year."*)

As for the Topsham River Commissioners, the 1840 Act provides for a body of 7, of whom 3 are appointed by ECC each year and 4 of whom are elected annually from local Topsham inhabitants, as set out in Clause 22 of the 1840 Act, *"being respectively owners or part owners of vessels trading to the Port of Topsham aforesaid, or being respectively rated to the relief of the poor of the parish of Topsham aforesaid at the yearly sum of twelve pounds or upwards...."*. The TRCs meet quarterly in General Meeting, with an AGM when the four new Topsham Commissioners are elected in Public Meeting for the ensuing Year, as prescribed in the 1840 Act. A copy of this formal notice, for the AGM 2022, is now inserted, in order to present the traditional form of words required.

Under Clause 30, the TRCs may *"appoint a fit person to act as their clerk during their pleasure, and to allow such a person a reasonable salary for his time, trouble and attendance in performing the duties of his office ..."*

Under Clause 31, there is an express power for ECC to *"cleanse and deepen the channel of any part of the river Exe, from the said city of Exe to the high sea, and to preserve and improve the navigation of such river in such manner as they shall think proper, and for the purpose aforesaid to dig up, prostrate and destroy all manner of weirs, rocks, sands, gravel, and other lets and nuisances whatsoever in the said river"* [This Clause repeated the powers granted to the Chamber by the River Exe Act 1539]

The Exeter Port Dues Bill was read a third time and passed on Tuesday 2 June 1840.

EXETER PORT DUES.

AN ACT

FOR

Equalizing, defining and regulating the Petty Customs, and for facilitating the Collection thereof and of the Quay Dues payable to the Mayor, Aldermen, and Burgesses of the City and Borough of *Exeter*, and for preserving the Navigation of the River *Exe*.

3 VICTORIA.
SESS. 1840.

Heading of Exeter Port Dues Act

In the PARISH of TOPSHAM

And in the Matter of the Exeter Port Dues Act 1840

PUBLIC NOTICE for the ELECTION of FOUR TOPSHAM RIVER COMMISSIONERS for the PORT of EXETER

We, the undersigned, being two of the elected Commissioners under and by virtue of the 22nd Section of an Act of Parliament made and passed in the 3rd year of the Reign of her late Majesty Queen Victoria, entitled an Act for the Equalising, defining and regulating the Petty Customs, and for facilitating the Collection thereof, and of the Quay Dues payable to the Mayor, Aldermen and Burgesses of the City and Borough of Exeter, and for preserving the Navigation of the River Exe, DO HEREBY GIVE NOTICE that the ANNUAL MEETING of the Inhabitants of the Parish of Topsham being respectively Owners or part Owners of Vessels trading to the Port of Exeter aforesaid, or being respectively rated to the relief of the Poor of the Parish of Topsham at the yearly sum of £12 or upwards, will take place at the Matthews Hall in Topsham aforesaid on MONDAY, the 7th day of NOVEMBER, 2022 at 7.30 o'clock in the Evening:-

> For the purpose of Electing Four Commissioners for the said Parish of Topsham pursuant to the Exeter Port Dues Act 1840: Be it Noted that the Present Commissioners are James Norton, Mark Mills, Eliot Wright & Godfrey Whitehouse, who go out of Office but are eligible for Re-Election and who have signified their willingness to so stand and continue in Office, if so elected.

Dated at Topsham this 7th day of October, 2022

Signed ....

Please Note: All enquiries regarding this Public Notice are to be addressed to The Clerk to the Topsham River Commissioners for the Port of Exeter, namely:--
Mr T R Epton at 25A White Street, Topsham, EX3 0AE e- mail: t.epton@btinternet.com

Published at St. Margaret's Parish Church, Topsham; Matthew's Hall, Topsham; Topsham Sailing Club.

Public Notice of Election of Topsham River Commissioners

CHAPTER TWO
The Historical Context

The 1840 Act was not enacted within some commercial vacuum or "bubble" but should be considered as a last link within an extensive chain of far wider events that embraced both local and national contexts, to the extent that it might be helpful to make general reference to national events, in order the better to illuminate the wider picture before focussing upon the *raison d'etre* for the local purpose and functions of the TRCs.

[A] The National Context (1800 – 1850)

The Country had recently emerged (under the Congress of Vienna 1815) from the burdens of the Napoleonic Wars, with their blockades of our European trading, whilst coming to terms with a fast-changing world of social, political, mercantile and technological developments, in which the Enlightenment and Rational influences were colouring the political and social landscape. These factors have been expanded upon in Appendix 1 to this Book, for those seeking a wider picture, against and within which the daily lives of the population of the City of Exeter and the Town of Topsham can be placed. In terms of the working or labouring classes, who were then forming the substantial bulk of the population of Devon, this Book seeks to give, "between the lines", a voice and words to the unheard – the lightermen, the bargees, the pilots, the quay, dock and port workers, the shipbuilders, the rope and block-makers, the skippers and their crews, together with their wives and families who constituted not only the backbone of the Port and its trading history but also the humanity through whose daily lives and toil can now be interpreted and distilled the history of Topsham Town as also experienced within all these wider aspects of the outside world, which are worthy of being included for the effect that they came to have upon the Port of Exeter and its commercial prosperity (once the hub of the City's wealth and prestige) and its future viability.

[B] The Local Context: -if this can be perceived as relevant in two main areas: -

<u>(i) The Port of Exeter as a Haven Port but one subject to the limitations of its own geography.</u>

As a Port governed by major levels of difference in the rise and fall of its tides, in particular with their Springs and Neaps, its Channel was hindered by shoals and banks from the Port entrance at Exmouth right up to Exeter Quay. It was a River that required pilotage and the deployment of lighters and barges for transporting, loading and offloading cargoes and ferrying them through shallower waters, often causing long waiting periods for the rising tide in The Bight anchorage downriver.

Entrance from the high seas into the Channel entrance itself at Exmouth was always a major hazard, as crossing the Bar depended on tides high enough to permit the particular vessels making passage, whilst the shifting sands of the Channel and at Dawlish Warren were an additional and constant peril. It was only through the efforts of Robert Davy of Topsham (1762–1862) that the Bar at Exmouth came to be first buoyed, with the assistance of Lord Rolle. Pilotage here was a necessity – and another expense, as also it was, onwards, upriver to Topsham Quay and then for another separate pilotage from Topsham Quay up to the Lower Sluice entrance to the Canal by way of the Tide-channel, also known as The Back Gut (see Chapter Three).

Apart from the long standing and close connection established in the Cod fishing industry between Topsham and Newfoundland, there arose, in addition, the increasing commerce and prosperity for the Port, particularly for the woollen trade exports and the import of foreign goods (such as wines, spirits, sugar and spices), plus local coastal cargoes including coal, with the result that vessels became more frequent in their voyages and numbers, as well as becoming of increasingly larger dimensions and of deeper draught, for carrying such larger cargoes, thus exacerbating the problems of negotiating the Channel at low tides (Neaps in particular), so that the general inadequacy of the River became increasingly apparent, leading to further and continuing efforts to improve and upgrade the canal to allow for all of such more demanding needs. It became a game of "catch-up", albeit doomed to eventual failure, but with Topsham Quay, as the "deeper Quay", to a degree holding its own, provided its navigation channel was kept properly dredged.

An important factor to be established early in this story is that Topsham Quay was a major "station" or the City of Exeter's Entrepot in its own historical and established right, for so many Cargoes coming in and Exports going out, with many goods (especially the heavier freights) being first unloaded at or shipped from Topsham Quay, with onward transport to or from Exeter Quay being by Lighter or Barge (drawing much less water than a bigger Vessel and so better able to cope with the tides and Tide-Channel/Back Gut to and from the Lower Sluice as well as the then depth of water available in the

Canal itself). Even this scenario is more complicated than stated because many Merchants, particularly the powerful Tiverton Wool Merchants, chose to use Topsham Quay as their trading Port in any event. It was not only from custom and habit but, for good practical reasons, in that their cargoes were so valuable that they did not want to risk damage in their transit from all the loading and unloading into Lighters for carriage to or from the Canal.

Also, it is important to keep in mind that many of the Vessels using the Port carried "split-cargoes" with some goods, especially heavier goods, destined for Topsham Quay for onward journey, whether to Exeter itself or often to other parts of Devon, whilst other less heavy goods (more suitable for Lighter or Barge passage) were meant for onward transmission via the Canal.

In parenthesis, this situation formed one of the commercial "prompts" for the Exeter Chamber to want a Ship Canal, designed with a capacity to take **all** Cargoes straight and direct to Exeter Quay, as will appear in Chapter Five.

Meanwhile, other ports in the Country with much better open and deep-water facilities started to develop in ways that made the Port of Exeter at increasing risk of becoming uncompetitive. The Golden Age *(1660-1760)* of the River Exe as the pride of Exeter's prosperity was over. Between 1800 and 1850 it became "marginalised" and overtaken by other ports. It seems not the case that the Port itself was tainted by the Slave Trade to the extent of Bristol or Liverpool, as opposed to profits derived from Slavery itself. *(n.b. The Voyage of the Slave Trader "Dragon of Topsham" in 1699 as referenced in "Topsham & Sugar" – a valuable Topsham Museum Research Project Publication – 2021).*

There was indeed a Topsham connection in certain families to the "Plantations" and the "Caribbean" and also there was a Sugar Refinery at Retreat, Topsham, which the Research Project has carefully explored.

(ii) The relationship between the respective Quays of the City of Exeter and of the Town of Topsham.

In earliest times when vessels were smaller and fewer in number, it is said that they could reach the water gate in Exeter itself. After the obstruction of the river up and beyond Countess Wear, by Isabella Countess of Devon in 1284, in the days of the Courtenay family's powers, the main quay for the port of Exeter was Topsham Quay. This caused the City's Chamber to construct the canal in 1563/1566, to provide a channel from the Exe up to the Exeter Quay, in competition (for convenience as well as in charging rates) with the road transport by packhorse and then wagon, involving the loading and unloading of goods at Topsham Quay. After running battles between Exeter's Chamber and Topsham merchants over port dues, an Act of Elizabeth 1 "indicated that Topsham was the legal landing place" which in later years was the subject of a compromise agreement between the two competing commercial quay interests in 1580. *(Reference with acknowledgement is made to the work of Mr Wallace T*

MacCaffrey, in his "Exeter 1540 – 1640" - Harvard University Press, 1975).

Allied with this historical tension, the ownerships, lettings, leases and workings of the two Quays seemed to become a "Moveable Feast", with their differing and various owners and lessees at various times and having their particular mercantile interests, such as the powerful Tiverton merchants in the woollen trade preferring to use Topsham Quay for their imports and exports, which two quays were often in basic conflict but also enjoined together by the umbilical cord of the Exeter canal (first in its Lighter Canal epoch & thereafter as a Ship Canal, in its own two phases of upgrading in 1725 *(Dr Oliver's Article)* and then, finally, in 1826), where matters rested until 1820 when the Navigation Committee of the Chamber (constituted in 1814) brought in James Green for his Reports in 1820 and 1824.

The two quays were as Castor and Pollux, twin stars in the Firmament of the Port of Exeter.

In Appendix 2, I have included the article upon the History of the early Navigation of the Exe by the esteemed Scholar and Antiquarian, the Revd. George Oliver, as published by the Exeter & Plymouth Gazette on 2nd October 1830.

[C] The Constructors and Engineers of the Exeter Canal

It appears common ground that the Engineers for the sequence of the canal works and up-gradings are as follows *(see References and Acknowledgements to Mr Kenneth R Clew's important & authoritative work)*. The periodic, continual maintenance and running improvements are not included in this list below: -

John Trew	Engineer & Gentleman *(n.b. Not a "rude mechanical" – he was granted professional status)* of Glamorgan (1563 to 1566) – for the first Lighter canal from Exeter Quay to Matford Brook, just above Countess Wear.
Richard Hurd	Engineer from Cardiff (1676) Improvements and ½ mile extension from Matford Brook to Trenchard's Sluice/The Lower Sluice.
The Interregnum: –	**William Bayley** from Winchester – (1698) who took the City's advance of finances and fled, leaving the Canal unimproved and in a state of disrepair and disarray.
Daniel Dunnell	(1699 to 1701) – with Voluntary help from the people of Exeter. within which period I would suggest (without dogmatism) the Tide-channel/ Back Gut was cut, as an artificial channel, between the Lower Sluice and its connection with the main Navigation Channel, just where Topsham Lock was to be later constructed. (A Gilbert

Greenslade is also mentioned in the respected Antiquarian Dr Oliver's Observations of 1826).

The **Chamber and its Navigation Committee** (1701 to 1824) – The series of improvements and repairs etc. Dr Oliver suggested that it was in the early part of 1725 that "the Port was opened" following new improvements, which brought trade and wealth for many years ("the Golden Years") to the Merchants of Exeter.

James Green (1824 to 1827) – The County Surveyor of Bridges for Devon – his reports to the Chamber in 1820 and 1824 are important documents, to be referred to later in Chapter Four.

CHAPTER THREE

The Lower Sluice & the Back Gut

The principal "bugbear" of the Canal had long proved to be the Lower Sluice, *(as the new Entrance to the River when the first Extension was cut from the old Entrance at Matford Brook)* with all its problems as a single pair of gates, rather than itself being a lock (see Chapter One – Provenance). It was also and originally called Trenchard's Sluice *(after Peter Trenchard, the first Lock-keeper)*. Its exit was connected by the River in its downstream passage to enter the Navigation Channel of the Exe at Topsham, initially by following the original Channel on the eastern side of the river (by "Retreat") as originally had been the navigable Waterway up to Exeter Quay before it became blocked by the various Weirs. Then, by 1701, the connection to the River was by means of the Tide-channel (the "Back Gut") (currently perceived by me as probably being fashioned under Daniel Dunnell's improvements, unless further researches might confirm that it had been included in Richard Hurd's earlier Improvements of 1676). This Tide-channel itself was the subject of shoals and banks and very awkward bends that required separate pilotage between Topsham Quay up to the Lower Sluice. It was a menace to navigate, even on the highest tides. *(See copy Plans referred to in the Maps Section at the beginning of this Book)*.

As the Chamber recorded

> *"The state of the navigation between the lower sluice and Topsham and the dilapidated condition of the banks in the tideway of the canal had for a long time engaged their attention. And being extremely desirous to remedy an evil which was generally complained of, and which, throwing great obstacles in the way of increasing trade of the port, was obviously detrimental to the general interests and commerce of the city, they undertook the extension of the canal from the lower sluice to Turf"* [Exeter Flying Post 26th October 1837].

The Minutes of the Navigation Committee (held at the Devon Heritage Centre) show the never ending problems and continuous costs of repairing, replacing and maintaining this Single Pair of Sluice Gates, to the point that it must be asked why, granted the early construction and technical success of the Double Locks Pound in mid-section of the Canal, no proposal for replacing the Lower Sluice Gates with a similar Double Pair of Gates and Pound was ever considered, until James Green suggested this as a final remedy in his First Report of 1820, although he then also thought and clearly expressed (whether as a Recommendation or an Afterthought, but in any event studiously ignored by the Chamber ever thereafter…for whatever reason…) that moving the whole Lock a little further downstream to the Navigation Channel at Topsham, rather than replacing the single Gates at the Lower Sluice with a Double Pair of Gates to create a pounded Lock, would have been the better solution, as well also as cutting out the miseries and limitations of the Tide-Channel/ Back Gut altogether.

This question has helped develop a key aspect of my Argument in this Book.

To particularise the general, it is useful to summarise the practical problems faced by the Ships, Barges and Lighters in navigating the Back Gut, with its approaches to the Lower Sluice from Topsham being shallow and every passage, whether of entry or exit, being wholly governed by the tides, winds, weather generally, the size of vessel and tonnage weight of its cargo which governed its ability to cope with the rise or fall level of the tide at the particular time for the transit of the goods in question. Whether art or science, the working experience of the Topsham Pilots and the Lightermen, hard won but so easily forgotten, was crucial in coping with this ever-changing daily scene.

As Vessels increased in size with heavier tonnage of their cargoes, Spring Tides became more vital. Starting at the Entrance to the Estuary (see Chapter Two - Historical) the larger ships began to find the 12 feet at HW Neaps on the Bar at Exmouth a first hurdle to overcome. By the 19th Century some large vessels were obliged to stand off the Entrance for nearly two weeks whilst once across the Bar large vessels might then have to anchor in the deep water of The Bight, awaiting sufficient water on a Spring Tide to reach Topsham and/ or then upriver to the Lower Sluice of the Canal via the Tide-channel with its own hazards and problems. The inevitable delays caused many cargoes to be split, either at The Bight itself or at other Ports upriver to Topsham Quay itself, for transfers to Lighters and Barges and then onwards to the Lower Sluice. At Neap Tides this need became a common practice, with the Bar at the Lower Sluice a constant Shadow over the whole pattern of working. In addition, the handling and re-handling of goods for transhipment added to the expenses of transport, apart from the risks of damage to the goods themselves.

The problem for the efficient working of the Canal was that the Lower Sluice was too far upriver and inadequate to *serve*

"The grand purpose of regularity and despatch of trade" and *"of little benefit to the inhabitants at large, inasmuch as it admitted only of the navigation of craft of a very limited tonnage. And therefore, fell short of the growing wants of the citizens and that degree of utility which was required".*

The two Reports by James Green in 1820 and 1824 form the basis of Chapter Four, next to follow, but in terms of the Tide-channel and the Lower Sluice it can be said that James Green found that on the sill of the Lower Sluice (with its single pair of Gates) there was only four feet of water at Neap Tides. Also, because of the intricacy and narrowness of the Tide-channel, between the Lower Sluice and the Main Channel of the River (at Topsham), all vessels had to take Pilots from Topsham, to navigate it. What made this more necessary was that the Tide-channel, narrow as it was, was obstructed by shoals, and by having no towing or tracking paths on banks, which were composed of soft mud. On the lower side of the Lower Sluice, the tide at Neaps seldom flowed more than six feet, and even their attaining that height depended very much on the wind. Vessels of a size usually trading with Exeter itself could, as a result, only enter at Spring tides, which averaged barely ten and a half feet of water, on the sill of this Sluice.

Besides these problems, the mode of construction of the Lower Sluice formed another and major impediment to the trade of the Canal, as Vessels could only traverse this Sluice by means of the natural flow of the tide, and Vessels drawing nine feet (the largest that could approach Exeter Quay) could not, even if assisted by the tide, pass up from the Lower Sluice to the Double Lock but were forced to wait until there was sufficient water drawn down from the higher level, in order to raise the pond level of the Canal between the Lower Sluice and the Double Lock to such a height as would enable them to pass up the Canal.

Vessels leaving the Canal had their own problems, which amongst others involved emptying the long section of water between Double Locks and the Lower Sluice in order to reach the level of the River in the Tide-channel, which could become choked with rubbish, as well as discharging the waters from the Alphington Brook, to prevent adjoining lands being flooded. In addition, the constant emptying of this section of the Canal gravely imperilled the stability of its supporting Banks.

Of the Tide-channel itself, it was not nor did it ever become the main Channel of the Exe. It was always an artificial Channel through which the tide ebbed and flowed and into which some of the Exe waters trickled through a shallow channel between sedge-covered islets *(a sense of what this pattern of channels looked like can be seen in the aerial photographs of the landscape, both before and then during the construction of the M5 Motorway over the River Exe in 1976/7).*

Despite being tidal, the Tide-channel in its designed and fabricated role as the Mercantile Channel to the City, did not have the beneficial scouring waters of the Exe flowing through it, to keep it cleansed and free of debris, making it susceptible to silting up, even if recognising some effect that might have helped, arising from the constant emptying of the section of the Canal waters through the Lower Sluice, as already mentioned.

Putting these two problems together, for the Vessels and their Crews, Lightermen, Bargees and the Topsham Pilots, it must have brought Odysseus into the mind of many a cautious Captain and Ship-Master as he left the warm bosom of Topsham Quay with his Charon-style Pilot to work the Passage, to face his own private Idaho of Scylla and Charybdis upstream, before reaching the Ithaca of Exeter Quay....

Topsham Lock, the Lower Sluice & the Back Gut

Aerial view of River Exe and Canal showing Back Gut and position of Lower Sluice

Aerial view showing Back Gut and position of Lower Sluice with modern motorway bridge.

CHAPTER FOUR
James Green & his Two Reports of 1820 & 1824

A Report was commissioned by the Navigation Committee for the Chamber in October 1820 from **James Green**, the appointed in-house Surveyor and Civil Engineer for the project and the County Surveyor of Bridges for Devon – a Member of the Society of Friends, a Quaker, *(en passant as opposed to the entire Exeter Chamber's Members having made oath to the rites of the established Church of England); ("the Ever-Faithful city," Alderman Robert Rogers Sanders, when repeating the words of the Earl of Bath in 1688 to the Commissioners in their Report into Exeter in 1834…),* to which Chamber, since the repeal of the Corporation and Test Acts, no Catholics or Dissenters had ever yet been admitted to become Members (per the 1834 Commission into the Exeter Chamber (see Chapter Ten and Appendix 8).

This First Report from James Green was sought *"for bettering the navigation"* and in its essential parts is set out in Appendix 3, being extracted from the Minutes of the Proceedings of the Institution of Civil Engineers, Transactions Vol. IV, session 1854 with its Abstracts and Appendices (this is the "**GREEN FIRST REPORT 1820**") which was rejected by the Chamber, for reasons to be explored in this Book, which in its Conclusive part raised a Case of by-passing (and then eventually closing off) the Lower Sluice by extending the Canal a little lower down-river and then recreating the Lower Sluice but, this time, with **two** pairs of Gates, *(i.e. as a proper Pound Lock)* to be built "<u>*somewhat further down the Tide-channel*</u>" *(my emphasis)* so as to join the navigation channel of the Exe at a place opposite Topsham *(indeed where the present Topsham Lock came to be constructed and which was the very place where the Canal if so extended there would run closest to the Topsham navigable channel).*

Thereby the Tide-channel /Back Gut could be avoided altogether. This could have been constructed within a moderate budget estimate for such works, well below that incurred in the Extension Works to Turf Pool. The consequences are set out in Chapter Ten under the Commissioners' Report of 1834 into the affairs of Exeter. The Green First Report 1820 was received and so Minuted by the Navigation Committee on the 21st October 1820 (NC .066).

What this First Report advised for immediate action, as major improvements since the last substantial improvements in 1698/1701 were: - (here included as the relevant extracts)

1. The Lower Sluice should be rebuilt, on its existing site, as a proper pounded Lock with (*n.b. at long last*) double pairs of Gates, where the cills would be dropped to the level of the River bed of the Tideway Entrance Channel.

2. The whole Canal should be deepened to a uniform depth of 10 feet.

3. Improvements to the Double Lock *(positioned between the Lower Sluice and the King's Arms Sluice at the Exeter Quay head of the Canal)* which was playing a key role in the successful operation of the Canal, as well as of a width enough to take two Ships at the same time.

4. The Alphington Brook problem and any other streams flooding into the Canal, when draining from the adjoining lands, should be re-directed back into the River by way of culverts or pipes built under the Canal to take their flows.

5. Then, as either a Suggestion or Recommendation, he included the express idea that rather than continue to be faced with the problems of the Tide-channel from the Lower Sluice, with all its continuing obstacles of nature (including shoals, winds and low Tides) and rubbish, apart from the extra expenses of Pilotage from Topsham Quay, that a wholly New Access could be created "*somewhat further down the Tide-channel*" at the point giving better access to the navigation channel at Topsham where the River ran closest to its Western Bank *(which would have been just the very site where Topsham Lock came to be built)*.

For reasons to be considered next, this Green First Report 1820 was rejected by the Chamber in favour of a Revised scheme of a vastly more expansive (and to be proved expensive) nature.

Then came "**the James Green Swerve**" 'twixt 1820 and 1824.

In terms of the Chamber's Budget for the City, so far so good, with James Green having reported the existing defects in the Canal, which might well have been tolerated for a Century or more but which by all accepted accounts had become inadequate for the Mercantile needs of the 19th Century.

The Chamber now wanted more and greater improvements than had been engaged in the First James Green Report 1820, with James Green being faced with the demand, not for a standard depth of 10 feet throughout the Canal but rather a depth to cater for Vessels drawing 12 to 14 feet of water as Ships and Tonnages increased in size and cargo-hold volume, year on year, to serve ever increasing regional populations which were becoming engaged in more industrialised forms of commerce. Also, the Turf was circa two miles nearer to the Estuary at Turf Pool than the existing old entrance at the Lower Sluice.

The James Green Swerve is a vital part of my Argument, whatever the reasons and the politics behind it. Somewhere, as events were to prove, there was a rationale behind the First James Green Report 1820, where his budget estimates might well have held up, whereas under the Second Green Report 1824 a flight of fancy seems to have taken over, with unfounded assumptions made about the "generosity" of the affected and grand landowners and their "demands" for the giving over of their lands for the Extension.

Further, this extended project was conceived without any preliminary soil investigations, cost/benefit comparisons, reflective thoughts by the whole Chamber including general consultations with the inhabitants of Exeter (as had happened in 1698) or any financial analysis being sought or aired. No open market tendering or priced Contract was considered, whether or not James Green had represented that from its contractual nature generally, no substantial and competent persons as contractors could be obtained for the Project, with the result that all was left to James Green's own superintendence and his professional authority, which was understood to be a sufficient sanction for Mr William Crockett as Treasurer to make his *(later deemed unauthorised)* payments for the Works as they proceeded. One has to wonder whether James Green was having to respond to higher authority (i.e. Messrs Crockett and Sanders on behalf of the Chamber) rather than being the "persuasive tongue" that carried weight with the Chamber. As a Quaker in the 1820's it does seem to me highly unlikely that he was leading these decisions in some arbitrary fashion, with which William Crockett meekly went along. In his private world, everything was achieved by "consensus". That was his ethic.

The Confirmation of the recommendation of the Canal Extension down to Turf Pool, as set out in the Green Second Report 1824, was given by the Chamber on the 21st February 1825. There are gaps in this sequence of events that remain obscure. Whether this "Swerve" was seen by the Chamber, with its unelected oligarchy of professional Gentlemen and wealthy pillars of Society in the City, in its own right as the preferred technical solution to remove the acknowledged and agreed problem of the Lower Sluice or whether it was seen as a major chance or opportunity to score historical points over the "Traders" and Merchants of the Town of Topsham is an interesting aspect that, within the eternal mysteries of our English Class structure that passeth all understanding, is perhaps no longer left as an Open Question; one which will be referred to later in Chapter Nine "Hubris and Nemesis".

It does seem that all the Members of the Chamber themselves were not given a full and balanced appraisal of both the technical and also the political aspects of their decision, granted that Topsham Quay was to be by-passed. At that point, on the part of the Chamber, the financial consequences of their decision would not have been anticipated, in part because of the rush to start the Extension and in part because of the influence of their two key Members,

Messrs William Crockett and Robert Rogers Sanders.

However, accepting that the main question to be confirmed is whether the rejection of the Green First Report 1820, at least in respect of any Extension *"somewhat further down"* the River from the Lower Sluice, was wilfully resolved on the part of the Chamber or, to be generous, was overtaken by the fever of events (or an active imagination) it is the case that the Extension to Turf Pool was implemented under the aegis of the strong personal convictions and influence of these two leading Citizens of the City and the most powerful personalities in its governance through the Chamber. In foremost position came Alderman William Crockett who was appointed, or became the self-delegated "Executive Manager" on some more informal basis, the Treasurer of the Canal Extension project, responsible for Receiving the Funds for the Project, and whose somewhat "informal" methods, if any, of acting as the Payments Comptroller accounting for their Dispersal (such as being aided by the evidence of Receipts, Vouchers and Dockets) came under close scrutiny when the financial disaster unfolded and the whole Chamber became involved in the inquest (see Chapter Nine and Appendix 7, with one of the Western Times Press Reports headed up as "A Can of Worms").

William Crockett was a Brewer and Wine Merchant, of sufficient standing to be considered "professional" rather than "trade", whose Brewery came to supply the Beer for the navigators of the Works (which also led to further enquiry later, as will be explained). He was aided in strongest support by Alderman Robert Rogers Sanders, a prominent Member of the Chamber and an Exeter Wine Merchant of undoubted professional status who joined the Navigation Committee on the 18th April 1825, when the Extension Works were in full swing, and who was the Mayor of the City at the time of the Grand Opening of the Extension Works on the 29th September 1830. His Speech in Reply on behalf of the Guests at the Public Dinner held at *Congdon's Royal Subscription Rooms* is included in Appendix 6.

There is a sense in all his recorded words that he had, perhaps, a somewhat developed sense of his own majesty. Mayor Robert Rogers Sanders remained an unqualified apologist for the Canal Extension Works despite the dire financial results for the City, which resulted in the Canal Extension Act 1829 being enacted, as being an "escape route" out of the problems which the Extension had created, with its potential personal liabilities to be faced by the Members of the Chamber.

It is important to note that my Argument is addressed to the issues being explored and not to the personalities involved. I am making no suggestion in any way that the individuals who now enter the picture were in any way personally dishonest or acted other than in accordance with their own strong convictions and beliefs (even if in the event such proved misguided!).

I also mention that sometimes I have equated the Chamber with the City of Exeter but this was before the Municipal Corporations Act 1835 transformed the whole system of Local Government in the Country. This is because until 1835, the Chamber was in effect an unelected Oligarchy of the "great and the good" of the City who considered that they were not answerable to the public at large (see Chapter Ten and various Press Reports – and also Chapter Two and Appendix 8).

At times, I have also found it difficult to trace the balance of responsibilities and powers of decision as between the Chamber on the one hand and the Navigation Committee on the other, recognising that Robert Rogers Sanders was a powerful figure in both, with deemed full knowledge of everything.

To understand the "Voice of the People" throughout all these events, I have relied upon the very extensive Press Reports of the time, which contain voluminous details of events and proceedings, with shorthand writers heavily engaged in reporting both facts and opinions to a standard and level long lost to our modern local Press. Law Court proceedings in particular received scrupulous attention to detail and are accepted as reliable for the accuracy of their reportage.

Another factor to appreciate is that James Green was only the in-house "Servant" to the Chamber for these Canal Works purposes. Even though a full professional in his own right, as a member of the The Institution of Civil Engineers, he was a "technician" in function and not part of Exeter's grander Society. Being a Quaker was evidence enough of his "place", in the Chamber's Church of England's "terms of being elected". He was under Orders from the Chamber, either directly or through the Navigation Committee. There was to come a "name and blame" conflict in the subsequent inquest about the financial disasters for the Canal Extension to Turf, with James Green being called to severe account for his estimates and budget and with Alderman Crockett having to explain his own role, including his accounting which, however honest, raises eyebrows as to its competence (see Chapter Nine - Hubris & Nemesis). The power balance between James Green and Alderman Crockett clearly rested in favour of the Alderman, in terms of who was the prime cause of the catastrophe.

The discussions between all parties make for uncomfortable reading when an attempt was made to establish who was responsible and who took responsibility. Whatever the post-mortem judgments, after 1835 when the new Local Authority regime was established, there were no sanctions or penalties levied or sought against any of those of the Chamber involved in the debacle. It might well be argued that they had a fortunate "escape" from their responsibilities and imprudent actions, if the latter were not actually viewed as misdemeanours worthy of criminal prosecution.

However, be all things as they may, James Green was duly instructed by the Chamber to prepare a Second Report in March 1824 (this is the "**GREEN SECOND REPORT 1824**") which would close the Lower Sluice completely and then extend the Canal straight down to Turf Pool, thereby by-passing Topsham and Topsham Quay and their Navigable Channel altogether. Whether this wish by the Chamber to divert trade from Topsham Quay to create a direct link between Exeter Quay and the Turf Pool was by calculated design of the Chamber or by "benign oversight" appears from my researches for this book to speak more for the former than the latter (See Chapter Ten). Old rivalries involving both Quays and Personalities can run deep in the Hearts of Man. ...

In following this revised plan, there is an absence of evidence that the Traders of Topsham were ever consulted in advance – nor had ever known of the First James Green Report 1820. If it had been known, then the Mandamus Case for Robert Davy would have been pleaded differently, to good effect in the arguments of Sir James Scarlett KC, for Robert Davy and his 4 colleagues.

At this point one must ask what role the Chamber had in this extension of the whole Contract to include Turf because the Minutes of the Navigation Committee are wholly silent and whilst there had been Minutes regarding James Green's First Report of 1820, there are none relating to his Second Report of 1824. This could reinforce the case that the concept and planning of the "Turf Dream" had been taken over by the Chamber, or rather by one or two of its prominent Members, meaning William Crockett, with Robert Rogers Sanders, in support. The evidence suggests that the Chamber as a body were content to delegate the whole Project to the management of William Crockett. That is how the finances came to be so mismanaged without interim questions and furore.

Suffice it to say that, in so pressing ahead in 1824/1826 to convert the Lighter Canal into a full Ship Canal, the Chamber created a financial disaster, resulting in turn with the enactment of the Canal Extension Act 1829 - but that only after the Robert Davy Case which is now the subject of the following Chapters.

As the Green Second Report 1824 does not concern the issues about Topsham Lock there is no need to proceed with it any further in this Book, other than references to Thomas Telford's involvement in his approval of the Extension Works to Turf as carried out under the 1824 Report, in respect of and solely based upon the Instructions he was given by the Chamber to provide his professional Opinions.

When becoming concerned about the benefits of the Extension to Turf, the Chamber had invoked the support and Reports of the renowned Engineer Thomas Telford, who had been commissioned to provide two overviews and endorsements of the Works accomplished – those being solely for the Extension Works down to Turf. With my own past in the law, a question quietly arises, namely - Who gave and what were the Instructions so given, to Thomas Telford, to produce his Reports? I can find no evidence or reference that he was ever told about the Green First Report 1820, still less asked to comment upon it, but suggest that he was only instructed upon the Green

Second Report 1824.

In professional terms, an Adviser only ever responds to the actual Instructions received – they do not "speculate" on other matters that might or might not occur to them or could have been relevant to the Instructions in hand. So, if this conjecture stands correct, Thomas Telford was never asked to compare and contrast the two Reports and so never did so. The moral: before assessing any Opinion, always ask to see the Instructions given, and by whom: First – from whence and whom cometh the Instructions? Thereafter follows the wisdom.

Thomas Telford was asked to provide two Confirmatory Reports upon the wisdom of the Canal Extension to Turf, which he gave on the 1st March 1824 and the 31st July 1824 (*which are included in the Abstract of the Proceedings of The Institution of Civil Engineers of 1845*) but neither make reference to the First Green Report 1820 and so are not included in the Appendix 3 extract.

It is worthy of note that, in the Davy Case in 1828/9, the very lengthy Affidavit affirmed to by James Green (as a Quaker) makes no mention whatsoever of his 1820 Report nor of the extension option to Topsham, but speaks lengthily about the recognised problems of the Lower Sluice and the Tide-channel/Back Gut, which was common ground between the parties and not in dispute per se. Nor does he mention or "volunteer" the possibility of having **two** Locks, the one at Turf and a new one at Topsham. That was left for the Bench to pick up during the Case. However helpful that might have been, it was not deceit or concealment by James Green or the Chamber but simply that the Chamber were only defending the facts of the Case as brought against them, namely that they should be ordered to re-instate the Lower Sluice as it had been in its original position. He would have been "advised" upon the required content of his Affidavit when drafting it and to only include the minimum of what was strictly necessary but not to venture outside his brief.

In the following events, the Extended Canal was opened on the 15th September 1827, as the old Entrance at the Lower Sluice then was closed off for all time. The new Canal Basin for Exeter Quay was completed 3 years later.

To complete his Engineer's role, James Green produced plans for the new Topsham Lock (following the Davy Court Case and Agreement and the enactment of the Canal Extension Act in May 1829) on the 7th October 1829, for inspection by the Navigation Committee. The Lock was completed in 1832.

In October 1837, with the inquest upon the Extension events in full flight and the new Council's concerns and questions requiring answers, the Council was referred again to the several questions asked of Thomas Telford in 1824. The main relevant question that Thomas Telford was asked to answer by the Chamber, apart from the quality of the works being executed in a proper and substantial manner, was:

"Whether or not the construction of a complete lock, with upper and lower gates, <u>in the situation in which the lower gates of the canal are placed</u>, (i.e. the Lower Sluice Gates) would not have answered equally as good a purpose to the canal, as the extension of the canal to Turf, by which a vast expense would have been saved to the Chamber? - Answer: I am of opinion, that making a lock <u>where the lower gates are now placed</u>, would not have answered the purpose of a perfect navigation up to the city of Exeter. On the contrary, that, besides having been subjected to the obstacles in the lower part of the river, (i.e. the Shoals and the Tide-channel between the Lower Sluice and Turf) the entrance itself would most probably have speedily silted up: and, therefore, that this project is quite unadvisable" ...

Of Topsham Lock, the Sherborne Mercury reported on the 11th June 1832 that it was completed, and *"several vessels last week passed through it into the Canal on their way to Exeter."*

The Exeter Flying Post reported having learnt with great pleasure that on the 23rd January 1840 *"no less a number than 583 vessels and craft that passed in and out of the New Canal Lock, opposite the Town of Topsham, during the past year".*

As for James Green, born in 1781, he died on 15th February 1849, aged 66 years - *"an eminent and distinguished civil engineer, - intimately connected with the City of Exeter and County of Devon for 35 years".* At the time of his death, he was the oldest Member of the Institution of Civil Engineers (which was founded 2 January 1818).

CHAPTER FIVE
The Canal Extension Act 1829

Suffice to say that, in so pressing ahead in 1824/1826, to convert the Lighter Canal into a Ship Canal, the Chamber created a financial disaster, which in turn resulted in the Canal Extension Act 1829. The works for this Extension were pressed forward by the Navigation Committee and/or the Chamber directly under the quasi or perhaps self-delegated stewardship as Treasurer of William Crockett – but with no budgetary controls in place, nor any cost/benefit analysis to compare the two schemes in the two Reports of James Green, no open competition in the market place for competitive Tenders, (the works being carried out "In-House" by the Chamber), nor seemingly and questionably with the full and continuing approval of the Chamber itself - and quite clearly, in the absence of any contrary evidence, after having carried out no consultations with the Topsham merchants and traders, who had their mercantile reasons not to be best pleased, apart from the historical rivalries between the City Quay and the Town Quay.

In the subsequent Court Case, no attempt was made by Counsel for Exeter to suggest that advance discussions had either taken place or had even been necessary, because he simply pleaded that the Topsham Traders needed only to go back downriver from Topsham Quay in order for their Vessels to enter the Canal at Turf Lock instead of advancing upriver to the Lower Sluice as previously. Apart from the extra expenses and tolls, this was ingenuous perhaps but unacceptable to Topsham.

In fairness to James Green, as highlighted in his Report to the Navigation Committee on the 12th December 1826, in seeking to justify, as best he could, the vast increase in costs incurred by extending the Canal to Turf, there were very considerable unforeseen costs in that length of the canal between the Lower Sluice and Topsham known as "The Slab" which would have been incurred in any event had the initial proposal in his First Report of 1820 been implemented in closing off the Lower Sluice and constructing the lock at Topsham, rather than pressing on to Turf. Be that as it may, the budget on a cost/benefit basis would have been more manageable and within the comfort of the Chamber in the light of the advantages that this First Report of 1820 envisaged.

To cover their personal exposure and prospective legal liabilities, the Chamber sought to secure an indemnity for themselves by securing statutory authority for financing the substantial losses incurred by the Chamber, by way of the issue of Bonds and taking out of Mortgages. Its Members in 1829 *(per Minute of the Navigation Committee dated 9th February 1829)* promoted a Parliamentary Bill for the (retrospective) statutory sanction of the Improvement Works under the Canal Extension as already completed and for their financing, including by intended effect an indemnity for themselves, as a sense of their being exposed to the legal consequences of their actions was becoming recognised by the inhabitants of Exeter (The contemporary Press Reports are evidence – per Appendix 7). However, in so doing the Chamber had not taken into account the "feelings" and interests of the Topsham merchants and traders in having their Quay by-passed (with the loss of Quay dues to Topsham) when the Lower Sluice was blocked off against any further role in serving the Canal from the Navigable channel up to Topsham and then by the connecting Tide-channel/ Back Gut, despite all its recognised hazards. The Pilots from Topsham Quay would also be fearing for their very livelihoods, as also the Town's Lightermen and Bargees.

It cannot be emphasised enough that the Chamber were becoming desperate to have the Canal Extension Bill enacted as soon as ever possible. This meant that they were on the Back Foot if any events were to delay or put their Bill at risk, such as a Law Suit, which could delay matters inordinately and would be a cause of even greater expenditure by the Chamber, as well as leading to much greater exposure of their misdeeds and improvidence. The Chamber could brook no delay. This factor had consequences very shortly, as happened in the first quarter of 1829.

To be noted now, the "leverage" which came to benefit Robert Davy in his negotiations with the Chamber, to settle his litigation was not to be underestimated and will be further explored in Chapter Eight ("the Agreement").

In the tumult that erupted when this dire financial situation came to light, the local Press played an invaluable role in publishing the concerns of the inhabitants of both Exeter and Topsham from their respective perspectives.

As reported in the Western Times on the 10th January 1829, a General Meeting was held in Exeter on the 9th January, pursuant to notice, to receive the Report of the Committee (of which Robert Davy was an elected Member) appointed to watch over the interests of the inhabitants, in respect of the intended Application to Parliament by the Chamber, for a Bill to regulate (with powers to increase) the tolls, of the new Canal, as well as providing Indemnity for the Chamber against the personal liabilities of its Members for its actions. This Report stated that the Answers given to the Committee by Mr H M Ellicombe (the City Chamberlain and Attorney & Solicitor) on behalf of the Chamber were *"anything but satisfactory"*. Also, that *"As respected Topsham no alterations whatever were intended"* (in the Bill as then drafted. i.e. either to reinstate The Lower

Sluice or to construct a new Lock opposite Topsham) – which thus sustains my Argument that, without the Agreement, of the 26th March 1829, Topsham Lock would never have been constructed and Topsham would have remained by-passed by the Canal Extension for ever thereafter.

The Committee regretted that their conciliatory Requests to the Chamber had been *"treated with such apparent contempt"* The Committee then resolved to suspend their functions.

A further article in the Western Times of the 21st February 1829 is very illuminating on the "Politicking" that had been going on, which involved, once again, those two Gentlemen, Messrs. Crockett and Sanders, who were revealed as having been "on manoeuvres" for their own reasons without the whole Chamber necessarily having known what they were about. Before reciting the Article, it is important to keep in mind that at the same time that the Canal Extension Bill was being pursued in Parliament, the Court Case in the King's Bench of the High Court upon the Rule for a Mandamus as obtained on behalf of Robert Davy and his fellow four traders in May 1828 was coming towards its Hearing at the same time, in February 1829 (Chapter Seven). At the same time, the Chancery Suit of the Chamber v. Robert Davy was also being carried on, in relation to the Broad (per Chapter Six to follow).

The Article in the Western Times dated 21st February 1829 makes for very interesting reading, viz: - "Exeter Local - The Canal

> *The chamber of Exeter cut an extension of the canal, and expended an immense sum of money in works, which in their judgment, and without consulting the inhabitants, might be for the benefit of the city, and having completed part of their work, and done that which they admit is illegal, seek from parliament an act to indemnify them against any prosecution for such misdeeds. The inhabitants of Topsham commence legal proceedings, for a restitution of the rights of which they have been deprived, and the inhabitants of Exeter meet to assert their objection to the enormous tax imposed on them. A gentleman of St Thomas volunteers, without any authority, to call on Mr Sanders and Mr Crockett, the two governors of the chamber, for an explanation, and Messrs Sanders and Crockett assure him, that unless the inhabitants of Topsham succeed in their application for a mandamus, they (i.e. the Chamber) will not go to parliament, and that the citizens may be perfectly easy".*

[Interim Note - The NC p.219 on 9th February 1829 had approved the draft Bill as produced by the Chamberlain and required him to proceed in soliciting the proposed Bill in London – i.e. before the Mandamus Court Hearing on the 11th February but despite the earlier NC Resolution on 1st January 1829 that

> *"the further consideration of the Bill be deferred until **after** the next term when*

> the *"Argument for the Mandamus is fixed and that such Bill be not finally settled by Counsel till the result of the application for the Mandamus against the Chamber to restore the Sluice Entrance may have been ascertained"*

Mr Sanders had become a Member of the NC on the 18th April 1825, NC p.143, and was fully apprised of every matter going on or arising for disclosure]

> *"The gentleman of St Thomas attended the meeting of the inhabitants, and stated the conversation he had had with Mr Sanders and Mr Crockett, and they were perfectly satisfied of the honor and integrity of these two gentlemen, who spoke as by authority, and thus the anxiety of the inhabitants was lulled into apathy. The result of the last week has been, that the mandamus is refused, and we naturally expected that Mr Sanders and Mr Crockett had spoken correctly, and that the chamber would not apply to parliament. But we hear, they now say, that the communication of Messrs Sanders and Crockett was only demi-official; and the fact is, that the agents of the chamber are gone to London, to obtain an Act of Parliament, which may seek to establish an enormous tax on the inhabitants for ever. So much therefore for the assertions of Mr Sanders and Mr Crockett. But we are told, they are merely demi-official.*
>
> *Our contemporaries, in the interest of the corporation, have reported the hearing of the mandamus, and that the judgment of the court was that the chamber had established their right to the canal. The respectable Editor of the Flying Post has stated it more correctly, and we, having the short-hand writer's notes, are enabled to give it still more fully, and to shew that the only question on which the court decided, was as to the form of proceedings, i.e. whether by mandamus or indictment, and determined that a mandamus would not lie, leaving the applicants to their remedy, by indictment. Not a word passed on the merits of the case, from the judges, except as to costs, and as each party has to pay his own, it must be inferred, that the bench thought the merits were against the corporation ...".*

The rest of the piece is a commentary upon the Chamber as a *"self-constituted body"* and that even if the Bill be

> *"made tolerably palatable to the inhabitants"* then if they will have *"received one breach of faith, we anticipate they will be cautious how they place most implicit confidence in their public trustees"* ....

As the financial situation became more exposed to public scrutiny, James Green found himself in a defensive situation, blamed as being the principal cause of this disastrous financial "adventure" whilst in turn relating to the strong influences under which he had laboured, especially those of William Crockett and Robert Rogers Sanders - those two significant figures in both Exeter Chamber and Exeter Society and its governance. In the nature of human beings, individuals might be forgiven for "running for cover" – for James Green, he invoked the support and Reports provided to the Chamber by the renowned Engineer Thomas Telford (see Chapter Four).

Reading the Press-reported contempt of many citizens at the *folie de grandeur* of the Chamber in having brought their City to near bankruptcy, it is comforting to find strong supporting views expressed from the time, rather than them being limited to my own analysis and conclusions, namely that the Green First Report 1820 would have met the budget restraints and practical improvements sufficiently to have justified any cost/benefit appraisal.

A piece in the Western Times of 4th April 1829 catches the situation exactly. It reads thus:

"Exeter Local - The Exeter Canal Bill has now proceeded so far through Parliament as to protect it from any effective opposition, and the clauses have been settled in the committee to the satisfaction of those who have deemed it worth their trouble and expense to guard their rights, and have manifested zeal sufficient to resist encroachment on their privileges.

The inhabitants of Exeter have felt sufficient confidence in their corporation, and have not even watched it in the committee. We trust they will not be disappointed on perusing it. But the inhabitants of Topsham have met the measure with determined opposition, and have fully succeeded in carrying their object – The Bill contains a clause which compels the Chamber to open the canal above Topsham, with every convenience for the passage of vessels.

This will be about a quarter of a mile further down the river than the old Lower Sluice, and at a more convenient place, because the channel of the river runs close to the bank. We predict that when the entrance is completed, four out of five of the vessels that come to Exeter will use it: first, because most of the traders have part of their cargoes for Topsham, and second, because they can sail up there, which will be generally more expeditious and save the great expence of additional hauling.

*This entrance will be more convenient than the old Lower Sluice, and we say that the people of Topsham have now shown the chamber what ought to have been the improvements of the navigation. **The extension thus far was all that was required**. Alphington Brook might have been carried under the canal as it is. The lock they are about to form would have pounded the water, and about £1000 or £1500 would have removed the shoals in the river, and the whole might have been completed for less than ten thousand pounds. The Canal produced a clear annual profit of £3000 and by this the expense should have been liquidated. But what is the result of the measures adopted; a tax is levied on the city of at least fifteen hundred pounds per annum, and that now fixed* *for ever on the public by an Act of Parliament. We have performed our duty, by frequently calling the attention of our readers to the measure. If they will not watch their own interests, it is their own faults.*

The Chamber of course have sunk their former surplus income in their calculation in order to effect this (as they consider it) public advantage. We think the Chamber must feel themselves indebted to the inhabitants of Topsham for thus showing them what would have been the better way of improving the navigation. How their own finances and revenue may be affected, we do not know, but the public, for whom they are trustees, ought to be informed.

The inhabitants of Exeter have placed implicit confidence in the Chamber, as to the scale of tolls, without any pledge, for the published scale was on the condition that the Chamber were not compelled to open another entrance. They have been compelled, and of course are now at liberty to introduce such a scale as they think proper. The only check, is the landing goods at Topsham, in case the tariff is too high, and this shows the importance of watching the interests of that port."

I suggest that such final question is the prescient one that eventually would lead to the Exeter Port Dues Act 1840, with its provisions to equalise the Quay/Town Dues. I also suggest that this contemporaneous Press piece fully endorses my Argument that the First James Green Report 1820 would have solved the very problems which needed remedy. It was all that was needed. The fact that it was overridden by his Second Report 1824 raises wider questions that might well touch upon the politics and mercantile interests involved between Exeter City and Topsham Town as well as the vainglory and superior ambitions of certain individuals, whose contributions to the best interests of the City perhaps be better left unspoken – (at least until Chapter Nine!).

The Canal Extension Act 1829 *[Cap.xlvii]* was enacted on 14th May 1829 *Anno Decimo Georgii IV.*

A Transcript of the relevant parts of the Act is included in Appendix 4 in which I have highlighted the Section in Chapter XLVIII, relating to the Reduction, Alteration, Modification or Regulation of the Tolls, Duties or Sums of Money, or of any or either of them respectively, so that their respective Rates shall not be raised or increased beyond the Rate thereof specified in this Act ,…

"and so that there be always one and the same Rate at the same Time for the "Ships, Vessels, Lighters, Barges, Boats, Craft, Goods and Merchandize respectively, from all Persons whatsoever, and whether the said Ships, Boats, Lighters, Barges, Craft, Goods and Merchandize shall enter the said Canal by the said new Entrance at or near the said Place called Turf or by the said intended Lock so to be made above the said Town of Topsham as aforesaid".

ANNO DECIMO

GEORGII IV. REGIS.

****

Cap. xlvii.

An Act for altering, extending, and improving the *Exeter* Canal. [14th *May* 1829.]

The "Banner" of the 1829 Act for extending Exeter Canal.

CHAPTER SIX

Robert Davy – Man of Topsham

As a preamble to the Man, the following Extract from the "Exeter Times" on the day of his Funeral, Friday, 10th September 1862, provides a setting for his place in this Book.

> *"All the people in Topsham may not know how the <u>old</u> corporation of Exeter came to construct the canal lock opposite the town. It was not their fashion to do the right thing, or anything right, unless compelled, and in this case, it was done as the result of a very expensive law suit, which ended in a compromise – Mr Davy finding the limestone for the walls at his own cost. and the corporation defraying the cost of construction."*

If nothing else, this is contemporary evidence that the relationship between Robert Davy and Topsham with the Chamber of Exeter was not of the easiest. His Court Case has many undertones, even if starting with the geopolitics that Exeter was a City and that Topsham was an independent and proud Town, with its own Charter from Edward I, and also that there had been much "History" between the City with its Quay and the powerful and regally connected Courteney family of Powderham, with its Quay at Topsham.

The question of our English Social Class structure should be considered also, in that the self-elected Members of the Exeter Chamber were of the County Gentry and pillars of provincial Society, Protestant and Anglican, whilst the Traders and Merchants from Topsham were part of a Working Port, with Dissenters in their midst (*witness the archival references at Topsham Museum in relation to the Quakers, Congregationalists and Methodists*). It is reasonable to ask if social and commercial snobbery might have entered into the history of their two Quays' mercantile rivalries, when, say, contrasting Mr Robert Rogers Sanders, Alderman and Mayor with Robert Davy, the businessman in Trade with all his multifarious enterprises. Once again, it is the story behind the story that adds colour and raises questions.

Robert Davy was an inhabitant of Countess Wear in the Parish of Topsham, who died on the 30th August 1862, aged 99 years and 10 months, having been born on the 20th October 1762. He was aged 66 at the time he brought the Court Case against the Exeter Chamber, together with four other local men whose names have not passed into local record. He was the instigator and sole funder of the Court Case which it is said cost himself personally over £800.

Robert Davy had been taken entirely blind in 1816 on his way to London by Coach, at the age of 54 years, following which he immediately underwent a series of gruesome eye operations, the first of which, on both eyes, failed completely. The second operation on his right eye, some two years later, partially recovered his sight until about 1822 before it began to fail again. He daily walked extraordinary distances and even when blind continued, guided by a boy, until his legs began to fail him in about 1840 when he was driven in a little four wheeled carriage. I mention this medical condition in the context of his Court Case in the years 1828/9 and as I consider his own motivation for funding the Case, having himself retired from Shipbuilding, at *Passage*, in Ferry Road, Topsham, in 1826 when he passed that business to his son Daniel Bishop Davy.

The extraordinary stamina, stoicism, astuteness and resolve in which he lived a full life in many areas of private business and public service are recorded in the archives at Topsham Museum *(as fully acknowledged with thanks in the References and Bibliography)*, with particular reference to his Biography in the form of a Memorandum written by his youngest son, Francis, about 6 months before his Father died, with a few notes appended after his death ("the Memorandum").

I also refer to the very helpful details given in the Topsham Museum Research Project *"Topsham & Sugar – connections with the Caribbean and Virginia"* (with the same acknowledgement and thanks) in its Chapter 7 - Topsham in Jamaica: The Davy Family and Chapter 11, Topsham Voices for Abolition."

These Archival References are essential reading for grasping the nature of Robert Davy and his achievements, having taken over his Father's business and then become a very significant Shipbuilder on the Exe, with numerous contracts for the Admiralty for Naval gun-brigs, bomb-ships and fire-ships to defend our Sea Lanes (and thereby, as the prime reason, our Colonial "possessions") as well as building large sailing ships for Trading, whether for Overseas or Coastal, including in particular a number of West Indiamen for trade with the Caribbean, (including the 500 ton *Jamaican Planter* costing at least £18,000 and licensed to carry 45 armed men – a Privateer?) but not Ships for the Slave-trade itself in its Middle Passage *(The Middle Passage was the stage of the Atlantic slave trade in which millions of enslaved Africans were transported to the Americas as part of the triangular trade)*.

A number of the extensive Davy family members themselves acquired or managed several Caribbean Plantations and therefore benefited from the mercantile results of slavery itself, as did Robert Davy. In addition, he built many "Scotch smacks" of 200 tons register, for carrying passengers and goods on the London to Scotland passage.

His father's business, as continued by him, was in building and repairing barges for shipping coal, culm and limestone upriver and from the Babbacombe area, of Torbay, where the family had quarries. Robert Davy himself started shipbuilding at Glasshouse before buying the property called *Passage* in Topsham, on Ferry Road, in about 1804 where he created his main Shipyard for building and repairing Vessels, to great success because of his reliability in meeting contractual deadlines and building Vessels to cost.

In about 1820 he started the trade of selling bar iron at Passage and also, then or soon after, started manufacturing chain cables and anchors. In 1821/2 he acquired the iron, hemp and tallow business of one Robert Rogers Sanders (*again this man appears*) at Palace Gate, Exeter, as well as the premises, starting his imports of hemp and tallow. In about 1825 he gave this business to his son Daniel Bishop Davy. So, from 1790 to about 1825 he was considered the West of England's foremost lime burner, coal merchant and shipbuilder, as well as being a substantial farmer at Countess Wear. Some trade with Newfoundland and as a Timber Merchant selling much oak timber and bark were yet further additions to his business empire, bringing his sons into partnerships as appropriate to keep it all within the family.

I have mentioned in Chapter Two that he was the initiator of having the Bar at Exmouth first buoyed, as the following further Extract in the Western Times in their Funeral Obituary dated 10th September 1862 pointedly states, viz:-

> *"There was a time when vessels could not come over the bar, and see their way in as safely as they can now. Mr Davy was the cause of having the Bar buoyed. He inserted a letter in … the Flying Post … calling public attention to the want of buoys, the late Lord Rolle, on reading the letter sent to him, and afterwards, rendered every assistance in carrying out the object. A letter was enough to move a lord, to effect an improvement: it required a law-suit to move a corporation"!*

The Memorandum emphasises that Robert Davy

> *"was solely the means of compelling the old Corporation of Exeter to erect the [canal] lock just above the ferry at Topsham. A very expensive course [court?] of law proceedings ultimately ended in a compromise, Mr Davy finding the stone. The going to law, together with the stone, must have cost Mr Davy at least £800".*

Apart from his own family business interests, Robert Davy was closely involved in parochial matters, principally in regard to the poor. Clara Place in Follett Road now stands in place of the Topsham Common Workhouse, which he had caused to be demolished in 1825, as being *"that costly nest of vice and dissipation."* He was elected one of the first Guardians of the Union in 1836 and hardly missed a Vestry Meeting when the applications of the poor were heard and then paid out. *"He always advocated the part of the poor, and was much respected …by all his brother-Guardians."*

At this point, it is pertinent to contrast the charitable and eleemosynary character of Robert Davy within Topsham Town, as fulfilled from his own funds, with that of Robert Rogers Sanders of the Chamber who, in the course of supporting the Canal Extension at such improvident cost, did not utilise his own fortune but rather was a principal party to the use of the Trust monies from two of the Exeter Charities of which the Chamber were Trustees - which Charities, *Atwill's Charity* and *Awliscombe Charity,* were for the relief of the Poor of Exeter…

I am not seeking to make this Book a saga of any personal Battle between Robert Davy and Robert Rogers Sanders but their contrasting social positions, businesses, personal authorities, and characters, when placed in conjunction with each other, seem to enforce the making of connections between their roles in how Topsham Lock came to be constructed, this being my sole purpose for writing this Book.

In his public life, Robert Davy was much involved with politics and world affairs, with much influence in Topsham, Exeter, Tiverton and Crediton (where the wealth of the Woollen Merchants had been established in the 17th and 18th Centuries). His own political position was set out in the Memorandum and deserves being quoted at length, viz:

> "He <u>discussed</u> public matters <u>freely</u>. He was a devoted Whig; and he lent a very great aid, both in person and purse, in the various hard-contested elections; and that too prior to about 1830 when men who took an active part, and expressed their opinions on that side of politics, were looked on very differently to what they now are. In those days they were almost despised, and called "Jacobites" and so on: Indeed, at one period they were obliged to be very careful how they expressed themselves, and were indeed at one time obliged to make themselves rather scarce."

Might this well not be a further distinction between Robert Rogers Sanders, as a presumed High Tory of the Exeter Chamber, in sharp contrast to the Whig Robert Davy of Topsham? Robert Davy himself was a faithful supporter of the Anglican Church and in regular attendance. Although buried in the Family Tomb in the Churchyard at Clyst St Mary, on the 5th September 1862 there is a fine Memorial Tablet to him on the North Aisle Wall of St Margaret's Parish Church in Topsham. A photograph of this Tablet is interleaved in this Chapter.

Whilst Robert Davy funded the Law Suit against the Exeter Chamber in the manner set out in Chapter Seven, next following, it is not known who were the other four Topsham men shown as being parties to the Action, their names not being found in the Chamber's papers as held in the ECC's Archive at the Devon Heritage Centre. Knowing Robert Davy's social concerns for Topsham Townsfolk, it could well be that he was prompted by the effect of Topsham Quay in having been by-passed by the Extension to Turf, upon the livelihoods

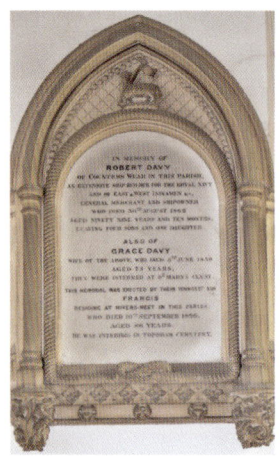
Memorial to Robert Davy

of all the local Lightermen, Bargees and Pilots, for whom regular work was essential for their already modest way of life and the precariousness of the Town's existence generally. Some of these men could have sworn supporting Affidavits along with Robert Davy himself. The affidavits sworn on behalf of the Exeter Chamber are included with their Case papers; Bargees speak only of the practical problems of coping with the Lower Sluice and the Back Gut.

To enquire further, beyond reasonable consideration, is mere speculation into the mind of Robert Davy. He had other reasons for seeking to discomfort the Chamber, to be explained later, in his parallel litigation in Chancery at the Suit of the Chamber against himself. He might well have seised the opportunity to exploit the leverage he espied relating to the negotiating weakness of the Chamber in being so exposed by their own financial difficulties following the Extension to Turf and their "rush for statutory cover" by a Parliamentary Bill, which both Chamber and Robert Davy must have known would be delayed by his Law Suit in seeking for a Topsham Lock to be constructed. The role of Messrs Crockett and Sanders in this area has already been revealed, when they seemed to promise one thing to the inhabitants of Exeter in their official capacity as the representatives of the Chamber which in the event proved "incorrect" but from which difficulty they had proclaimed that their intervention as having been only "demi-official" (Chapter Five – Western Times Article 21st February 1829) – an interesting engagement in casuistry. …

Robert Davy was a business man, whether blind or not, who had by conduct and his own money proved capable of protecting local public interests, even if, for himself, he might not have had any personal "skin in the game", as the dire jargon of a 21st Century Executive might present. But whatever his sense of committed public purpose, there is also the private sense of a moral prompt and purpose in his Law Suit because the Town of Topsham had not been treated "fairly" by the Chamber in its decision to extend the Canal to Turf Pool without any prior consultations with the Traders and Merchants using Topsham Quay. No such evidence of any consultation appears in the Court Hearing for the Mandamus, as the next Chapter Seven will indicate, by its very absence of any such reference in the Pleadings on behalf of the Chamber. Apart from this, however, Robert Davy did have "form" with the Chamber as will also appear in Chapter Seven. They were "known" to each other, even if not exactly, by any stretch of the imagination, bedfellows in some common cause.

CHAPTER SEVEN
Robert Davy v. the Exeter Chamber Court Case – 1828/1829

The Court Case – Robert Davy & 4 Others v. the Exeter Chamber - 1828/9, the Case being listed under the title of *The King v. The Mayor, Bailiffs and Commonalty of the City of Exeter.*

With the Green Second Report 1824 having been adopted and then being vigorously implemented through William Crockett on behalf of the Chamber, it became an immediate concern to the traders from Topsham Quay and the inhabitants of Topsham generally that the extension to Turf was designed to facilitate direct trade between the Bar at Exmouth and the City of Exeter, both for Imports and Exports, which would be at their own expense and disadvantage in being so by-passed.

There had been no prior consultations by the Chamber with the Town, and the Traders would not have been aware of the Green First Report 1820. If they had read it, it would not have been beyond the wit of Topsham Man to have spotted the original idea raised by James Green of moving the Lower Sluice a little further downstream, as a Double-gated pounded Lock, just opposite Topsham where the Channel runs closest to the Western River bank. Such a Lock would have removed the need to navigate the perils and awkwardness of the Tide-channel/ Back Gut, even if it removed the need for the separate Pilotage that the existing arrangements had required. By offering such an alternative, it would also have made a substantial addition to the force of the Claim that came to be pleaded in the following Court Case.

It was following this affront by the Exeter Chamber to the Port of Topsham and the likely fate for its continuing prosperity, that Robert Davy (1762-1862), the powerful businessman of Countess Wear and Topsham, described in Chapter 6, led a group of five Topsham traders in the year 1828 in the issue of legal proceedings against the City of Exeter in the King's Bench of the High Court by way of a Prerogative Writ of Mandamus, granted in the name of the King, on behalf of Robert Davy and the 4 others, seeking re-instatement of the Lower Sluice, but not stating it to be done at the expense of closing the Turf Lock, which had already been completed, in 1827. The claim made no demand for any alternative Lock, such as at the place where Topsham Lock is now sited. Nor was any reference to be made to the Green First Report 1820.

Once constructed and in use by 1827 the controversy over the Extension did not abate. Various letters published in local Newspapers set out the *folie de grandeur* of the Chamber's actions at the expense of Topsham, in such practical detail that they are important enough to be referenced in Appendix 7, where increasingly the Chamber was challenged in its trying to recoup its losses by varying the tolls being charged, for example in carrying out a commercial sleight of hand by shifting additional tolls upon Vessels and not on cargoes, thereby upsetting the toll on the old Canal at the Lower Sluice entrance at 5 shillings per vessel. One cannot overemphasise the power of the local Press in acting almost as a quasi-opposition in maintaining the principles of a democratic and open society, when set against an oligarchy of self-elected and powerful men with their own interests to be safeguarded. The Freemen of the City also had an important role to play in the governance and affairs of Exeter – as well as being exempt from payment of Harbour Dues! (to be further noted in Chapter Eleven regarding the Exeter Port Dues Act 1840). It was through the length and detail of the Press Reports that the groundwork was being laid in the public minds of both Exeter and Topsham inhabitants for the battle to come over the Canal Extension and the legacy of crippling Debt that these Works had imposed upon the Ratepayers of the City.

The reason for seeking a Rule to issue a Writ of Mandamus was one of procedural importance. It was the legal process way by which to act speedily and directly, in order to secure an early resolution of a matter, being one that could not brook delay and which would otherwise be obliged to engage the slower "Cart-Horse" wheels of the Common Law, with its Writs of Indictment, and, even slower, in a world of its own, the toils and risks of becoming "lost in Chancery" under the complexities of an Equity Suit. It makes for extensive reading in following the way in which the Courts were structured in England at that time, with their High Court in London in its several Divisions at the national level (such as the King's Bench, Chancery, Admiralty, Ecclesiastical for probates & wills and Court of Exchequer). With the regional Assizes, Quarter Sessions, and Petty Sessions there was a devolved form of administering Justice at local levels, whether regional or parochial.

The point of Mandamus as one of the Prerogative Writs was that it could bypass the slower procedures for bringing a Law Suit, it being issued in the name of the King, with the aim of advancing a very urgent object or forestalling something highly dangerous or prejudicial. To some extent, one might equate this concept as that lately developed, namely the law or practice of Judicial Review in the field of Public Administrative Law, in this case involving a challenge to some governmental action or proposed action or decision that is claimed to be unlawful or ultra vires. It seeks to "hold Government to account" – as did Davy's case, although in his Case there was a preliminary argument and debate about whether the Exeter Chamber were acting as private owners (of the Canal) or under the rules of public accountability for upholding a public right of navigation through the Canal, albeit on payment of agreed tolls, the Chamber having blocked up the original River passage and usage to Exeter Quay, whether by default (letting Isabella's Weirs stand) or by deliberate action (in commissioning Trew's Weir - 1563).

(As a comment, my relating a Mandamus to a present-day Judicial Review is in fact touched upon in a closing speech of Robert Davy's Junior Counsel William Webb Follett, who said that "here there is no remedy so effectual as a mandamus, particularly where one of the parties is a corporation".)

Let us revert to Robert Davy's claim. To be fair, he did not plead for a Topsham Lock to be fashioned that would be much better sited than the Lower Sluice with all its known problems, for reasons stated earlier that there is no evidence that he had ever read the Green First Report 1820 because it would have added to the strength of his opening Case, knowing that both parties were then at least agreed that the Lower Sluice had served its time and purpose and was ripe for being replaced elsewhere.

The other advantage, if not for the Topsham up-river pilotage with its long-established workforce of lightermen and bargees, of proposing such an alternative access to the Canal would have removed the need to maintain the Tide-channel/ Back Gut. It might also have compelled James Green to make reference to and expound upon his Green First Report 1820 when submitting his Affidavit as one of the Chamber's key witnesses. In the event, he was only required to rebut the Case as being pleaded, namely for simply re-opening the Lower Sluice. Also, always remember that when the Case was brought in 1828, the Canal Extension to Turf had already been constructed, in 1827. The Chamber were trying to dig themselves out of a hole into which their own improvidence had cast them… In a practical legal sense, the Chamber was on the Back Foot. The spade it was employing with such concern was its Canal Extension Bill, as earlier discussed in Chapter Five.

To be explained later, in Chapter Eight, it does make some sense in why and how the eventual Agreement dated 26th March 1829 was reached so quickly between the Chamber and Robert Davy, after the Rule was discharged, without the merits of the Case itself being heard and adjudged, despite the lengthy pleadings and arguments, by four learned Members of the Bar, on the 11th February 1829 and for which they were allowed the generous time, by Lord Chief Justice Tenterden at the end of a Law Term.

The Lawyers involved in the Case were favoured or privileged to be heard in the King's Bench by Lord Tenterden, a former British Barrister, and then taking the office of the Lord Chief Justice who served as the LCJ between 1818 and 1832 and by his colleague Lord Justice Bayley. For the LCJ to take this Case suggests that it carried a significance of its importance in the legal system at that time, because otherwise it might have been considered a regional or more local matter without any real wider or national context, whatever the Junior Counsel might have pleaded to the contrary.

Appearing for Robert Davy and his colleagues was Sir James Scarlett KC (1769–1844) an English lawyer of the Inner Temple, considered the then leading Member of The Bar, having taken Silk in 1816. He was born in Jamaica and was a prominent Whig in his politics until the Reform Bill of 1832, which he opposed. Later he became a Judge, as the Lord Chief Baron of the Exchequer. He had been the Attorney-General from 1827 until 1828 when there came a change of Government, but he resumed this office in 1829 until 1830, following another Government change. It was thus fortunate that he could accept the Brief in between such high political Offices thereby allowing Robert Davy to instruct the very best of Counsel, albeit at a Brief Fee to match!

As earlier noted, Robert Davy was also a committed Whig, which might well have had some bearing both on his choice of Counsel and also on his relationships with the Chamber, a majority of whose Members appear to have been outspoken and unequivocal Tories. Such differences would not have gone unnoticed at this local level…

As his Junior Counsel, there was William Webb Follett (1796–1845) of the Inner Temple and a fast-rising star of the Western Circuit between 1824 – 1830, having been a special pleader below the Bar from 1821 to 1824, when he was called to the Bar. His first Pupil Master was Robert Bayly. His (Follett's) place in the Town and its history is well established – he was indeed a Topsham Man.

Robert Davy's Attorneys in Exeter (details not yet found) appear to have instructed the Firm of Messrs Anderton & Scott as their Agents in London and by whom the Retainer for Davy would have been given to Sir James Scarlett.

Leading Counsel appearing for the City of Exeter was the Solicitor-General (SG), in view of a Rule for a Mandamus being issued in the name of the King. This does not mean that the then current SG had to appear in person, though he could do so, but usually he would be represented by another senior Member of the Bar. In this case, the name of Serjeant Welsh is referred to by the Chamber's London Agents, Messrs Walker & Coulthurst, in a letter to the Chamber's Attorney, H M Ellicombe, dated 11th December 1828, as having been given a "General Retainer" by them for the Case. He is never mentioned by his name in the Press transcripts of the Law Reports.

The Serjeant in the Courts was a very senior and highly respected Member of the Bar, with superior rights of audience in the Court of Common Pleas, before, over the ensuing decade, his role came to be paralleled by the emergence under Queen Victoria of the 'Queen's Counsel'.

(The very last Serjeant to be practising in the English Courts into the 1920's was Serjeant Sullivan, a former Member of the Irish Bar).

The Chamber's Junior Counsel was Sir John Taylor Coleridge (1790-1876), of the Middle Temple, who became an English Judge (nephew of Poet Samuel Taylor Coleridge) who was also a leading Barrister on the Western Circuit – and thus well known to William Webb Follett as both being Men of Devon.

To be further explained later in Chapter Eight, such connections might well explain how and why the eventual Agreement dated 26th March 1829 was reached so quickly between the Chamber and Robert Davy, after the Rule for the Mandamus was discharged at the Hearing on the 11th February 1829, perhaps indeed because of the very lengthy pleadings and Arguments heard at great length at the end of a Law Term, and having been allowed so much time to do so by the Lord Chief Justice.

So, to put it informally, this was a Case with "heavyweight Counsel" on both sides.

As to the mechanics of the Case itself, the Time-line can be briefly summarised as follows: -

First Step: Mid-May 1828 – Court of King's Bench - Exeter Canal

Sir James Scarlett moved *(i.e. applied for)* a Rule Nisi against the Corporation of Exeter, calling on that body to shew cause why the obstruction should not be removed which stopped up the entrance to the Exeter Canal, and that the Court without a moment's hesitation, granted the following rule: -

> *It is ordered that the first day of the next Term be given to the Mayor, Bailiffs and Commonalty of the City of Exeter, to show cause why a Writ of Mandamus should not issue directed to them, commanding them to open the old and accustomed entrance to the Canal leading from a place called the Lower Sluice, in the River Exe, above the town of Topsham, to another part of the said River, adjoining the said city of Exeter, to replace the Lock of the said Canal, at the said old entrance, and to allow ships to pass and repass through the said old entrance, at the place called the Lower Sluice, and through the said Canal to and from the city of Exeter, on payment of the same Tolls as have been heretofore paid Upon notice of this Rule to be given to the Mayor, and Town Clerk of the said city of Exeter.*

Second Step: Wed. 25th June 1828 - Court of King's Bench – Exeter Canal

Mr Coleridge moved *(applied for)* the Court to enlarge *(i.e. adjourn)* the Rule for a Mandamus obtained by Sir James Scarlett, and directed to the Chamber, directing them to open the old canal, which was shut up on forming the late extension. The Court enlarged *(adjourned)* the Rule until the next Term.

Third Step: 27th November 1828 – Court of King's Bench – Exeter Canal

By a Consent Order dated *"the Thursday next after 15 days of Saint Martin in the ninth year of King George the fourth (i.e. 27th November 1828)* (and after reading the several affidavits of the Witnesses for the Corporation) *and upon hearing Counsel on both sides and by Consent ...*

> *it is Ordered that the first day of the next Term be peremptorily further given to the Defendants to shew cause why a Writ of Mandamus should not issue directed to them commanding them to open up the old and accustomed entrance to the Canal leading from a place called the Lower Sluice in the river Exe above the Town of Topsham to another part of the said River adjoining the City of Exeter to replace the Lock of the said Canal at the said old entrance and to allow ships to pass and repass through the said old entrance at the place called the Lower Sluice and through the said Canal to and from the City of Exeter on payment of the same tolls as have been heretofore paid the said Defendants hereby undertaking to put the Prosecutors in the same situation as to the Trial; of any Issue or other Matter which may become necessary or be directed by the Court as if the Rule had been made absolute on this day And it is further Ordered that the Prosecutors upon the Motion to make this Rule Absolute shall be at liberty to read an Affidavit verifying the Act of King Henry the Eighth concerning the Amendments of the River Exe and Port of Exeter.* [i.e. this was to avoid having to formally apply to the Court to have the 1539 Act, even though an Acte Publicke, otherwise "proved" to be a true Act, admissible in evidence]. *Signed by Sir James Scarlett for the Prosecutors and the Solicitor General for the Defendants.   By Order of the Court.*

Fourth Step: 11th February 1829 - Court of King's Bench - Exeter Canal

This was the actual Hearing of the Case in London.

This Case, the Law Report of which is a legal joy to read in the eloquence of its language, its courtesies and meticulous attention to details, was listed under the title of *The King v. The Mayor, Bailiffs and Commonalty of the City of Exeter* and was heard on the 11th February 1829, in the King's Bench, Westminster, before Lord Tenterden, Lord Chief Justice and His Honour

Judge Bayley.

Although exhaustively pleaded by both parties, the Case was not decided upon, on its merits, as stated, for procedural reasons, namely as being "premature" and thus was the Rule obtained by Sir John Scarlett KC discharged.

Because of its brevity, the Judgement can be set out in full within this Chapter, with full relevant extracts of the lengthy Case Arguments made during the Hearing being contained in Appendix 5.

> *"Lord Tenterden. C.J - We think upon the whole that the Court must discharge this Rule – The first and principal question is, whether the public have a right to the navigation of this Canal into the River Exe? That is the first question, and that is a question which may be tried by Indictment against the Corporation for stopping up the entrance – that may be tried by Indictment. The other questions that may follow, may afterwards become fit subjects for the consideration of the Court, & if the public right be established, upon the trial of the Indictment, - which is the regular course – if the public right be so established, and if the interposition of this Court is then found requisite to compel the Corporation to that which they ought to do; namely to give the public the full benefit of that which belongs to them, it will then be time for an Application for a Mandamus, but at present we think the Application is premature, as the question should be first tried in the usual manner by Indictment. Rule discharged.*

This meant that future proceedings had then to be by way of a Common Law "Writ of Indictment", involving a hearing probably at the ensuing Assizes or some months or Law Term later. The history of the legal system and the Courts of law in the 19th Century is the fullest of subjects in its own right, but as was mentioned or hinted at in this Case, there was a practical hope (on the part of the Bench and all the parties!) of it never having to become a Suit in Equity under the Court of Chancery (a Dickensian world of the *"Ministry of Circumlocution"* - of another *Jarndyce v. Jarndyce*. It is vital to have read *"Bleak House"* if you wish to enter this legal World).

In the event, the Case never proceeded to a full Hearing on its merits, because practical heads prevailed and the Agreement dated 26th March 1829 between Robert Davy and the Chamber was signed, as set out in Chapter Eight.

In selecting Extracts of the Case Pleadings, the arguments in the Case regarding the Tolls formed part of the question of whether the Canal is a Private or a Public Canal and have been considered as not material to my own Argument. This is a separate Argument to the Tolls question, which related to the passing of vessels and cargoes, leading to the equality of Tolls as were to be set out in the 1829 Act. This was also one of the likely triggers for the 1840 Act with its further aim of establishing equality established between the Exeter and the Topsham Quays for the payment of Town or Quay Dues.

Without intending a spoiler, my legal instincts suggest finding "the guts of the case" in the Closing Argument of Sir James Scarlett KC as being the conclusive turning point, (forgetting all the wordy pleas regarding the Canal's status and all the exhaustive details about the tolls and charges, especially from Mr Coleridge as Junior Counsel to the Solicitor General), namely that the upriver section of the Exe from the Lower Sluice to Exeter Quay had been blocked up both by the Courteney family with their Weirs and by the City itself (John Trew's Weir - 1563/1566) against the provisions of the River Exe Act 1539, which were to maintain full unimpeded access from Sea to City.

The Chamber, in accepting these obstructions over such a long period, had overcome the navigation problems by having built their own first Lighter Canal from Exeter down by its initial line to the Matford Brook, then further downriver to the Lower Sluice. Thereby, the Chamber by its own free decision and conduct over such a long period of time, had **substituted** or replaced the usage of their private Canal (subject to an agreed toll) with that for **a public navigation** Channel, the effect of which had been to replace (whether by a quasi-dedication or estoppel[1]) the previous River passage from Sea to City and as a result the Canal had come to be used as of right in place of such previous rights as had been secured under the 1539 Act, but left unachieved or unenforced by the Chamber.

It was also made clear that Topsham was not hostile to Turf Lock as such, it simply wanted to get its own "Topsham Lock" restored to the *status quo ante*.[2] The force of these arguments, in my view, reinforces the belief of the Chamber being on the back foot in the legal argument, apart from their own background need and acute anxiety for speed in order to have their Canal Extension Bill enacted.

The fact that the Court made no Order as to Costs at the Hearing (i.e. each party was to bear their own) is highly significant in suggesting that Robert Davy's Case was accepted by the Bench as having merits to be pleaded, even if to be heard in a different Forum under another procedure, by Indictment (but anything other than an Equity suit in the Court of Chancery, which had been Sir James Scarlett's reason for his first move for a Rule of a Mandamus…).

I have been able to refer to the full manuscript transcript of the Case papers held by The Chamber *(DHC Ref: Box 21, Location G3/5/5/6)* as well as a full text copy of both the arguments and the Judgment as reported verbatim in the Western Times 21st February 1829. (Appendix 5). To date,

---

[1] *The term estoppel refers to a legal principle that prevents someone from arguing something or asserting a right that contradicts what they previously said or agreed to by law.*

[2] *The previously existing state of affairs.*

it has not been possible to discover the name of the other four Topsham Traders who were party to the case with Davy, nor indeed the copies of the Affidavits filed on their behalf.

Supporting my views about "Fragments" generally, it is an acknowledged problem when researching law cases such as the Davy Case that it is often the situation that the Solicitor acting for a private party does not keep their client's case papers indefinitely, nor, with clients' permission, consider placing them in a local archive. It is a County, City or Borough or other local body that so often is the "one-sided Custodian" of a Case's history – and outcome – as no doubt the Devon Heritage Centre might strongly confirm.

Often, it is the large-landed Estates who will either be maintaining their own Archival "Muniment Room" or be open to placing them on deposit in a local archive and research centre, which is of the greatest consideration and benefit for their successors, a real boon which deserves the fullest of appreciation and gratitude. I am generalising. There have been and hopefully always will be the honourable exceptions by the lawyer, with an historical cast of mind; whilst recognising that, in any event, Paper has given way of late to the Digital Age, with a new outlook required.

It must be stated, as a matter of good fortune, that despite the time constraints on the Court in 1829, the Lord Chief Justice Tenterden was prepared to hear all the arguments, though sternly "pleading" for no "repetitions" from the supporting Junior Counsel (John Taylor Coleridge and William Webb Follett). Something, at times, that I am not sure Mr Coleridge always fully observed!

Another aspect to this Case was the previous "form" or history of litigation as between the Chamber and Robert Davy, as already touched upon. They were "known" to each other….

Minutes of the Navigation Committee contain some of the story. For Example:

2 Jan 1815 "It appearing to this Committee that for a considerable time past Mr Davy at Countess Weir has not been called upon for the payment of dues for landing Coals, Limestone etc on his premises, which is considered from the extensive Trade he carries on, would amount to a considerable Sum annually. Resolved: - that it be recommended to the next Chamber to consider of the propriety of proceeding against Mr Davy for the enforcing payment of Dues on everything that he may in future land on any part of his Premises which may be situate within the Parish of Topsham".

14 Mar 1821 "And also to call on Mr Davy to show cause why he does not pay duty for all the coal and limestone landed on his premises at Wear".

Another substantial legal case was in hand, in Chancery no less, or had only recently been settled in which the Chamber were suing Robert Davy for having unlawfully extracted gravel and deposited materials on "The Broad" off Countess Wear, thereby imperilling the canal embankments and also causing shoaling in the river. Robert Davy had mounted a substantial defence, as the papers at the DHC reveal. This is yet another Case worthy of further research, but beyond the scope of this book to develop further.

There is the Minute of the Navigation Committee dated 7th May 1828 stating that

"The bank of the new canal just below the late lower lock (i.e. the Lower Sluice) on the eastern side having been undermined and thrown down by the increased flow of water against it in consequence of Mr Davy having taken away the gravel from Broad. This Committee beg to call the attention of the Chamber to the propriety of commencing an action against Mr Davy for the damages occasioned by his recovering the gravel above mentioned."

In this Case, Robert Davy was giving the most robust of defences, as Defendant at the suit of the City - a Topsham Man of Business &Trade, perhaps he did not show a respect to the Chamber to which they might have felt entitled, if not earned and with the underlying sense of being Davy's "betters"? Who can ever know?!

CHAPTER EIGHT

The Agreement dated 26th March 1829 -- Robert Davy & the Chamber

In the nature of things, after a Hearing and Order (as to the Discharge of the Rule for Mandamus and without any Judgment on the merits of the Case) such as the preceding Chapter Seven sets out for this Robert Davy Case, the Lawyers themselves might well confer, professionally, first with each other and then separately with their own Clients. Possibly also, I suspect from direct experience, with a "nod" from the Bench as well, noting Lord Tenterden's remark as to "**Let us have both is what they want**" referring to Robert Davy's position in accepting the existence of Turf Lock but wanting another Lock for Topsham as well.

In my opinion, on the facts of the Hearing itself, the Case looked "Ripe for Settlement". So, with all the post-Hearing inter-party discussions and "negotiations" then taking place, whether with James Green present or not (but doubtless with his Survey plans and suggestions available if not already to hand), the way was clear for "the Middle Way" to be negotiated. A resulting Settlement would avoid the further and embarrassing expense of another set of protracted Court proceedings for which the Members of the Chamber, now financially exposed and being desperate for a protective Canal Extension Bill to be passed at the first possible moment, were fearful of incurring yet further wrath from their fellow citizens.

Common sense makes it reasonable to conclude that this situation gave Robert Davy with his business acumen and status, an opening to exploit, namely "leverage" over the Chamber, which the Topsham traders and townsfolk would have well appreciated. In parallel with this Case, the two Chancery Actions were either imminent or afoot by the two Exeter Charities whose funds the Chamber had raided, improperly and unlawfully, to help fund the construction costs of the Canal Extension Works with consequent debts of magnitude. The ice was not only thin, it was beginning to crack and break. (The total Debt of £106,000 is referred to although a final estimate is referenced as reaching £120,000 - the Report of the Commissioners for Exeter 1834 in Chapter Ten).

In addition to Robert Davy's own role, the "hand of Follett" should not be discounted in explaining how the Agreement was reached so quickly. William Webb Follett was the Junior Counsel for Robert Davy and was a rising star on the Western Circuit (1824-1830) as also was John Taylor Coleridge, the Junior Counsel for the Chamber. With the leading Counsel Sir James Scarlett KC, for Robert Davy, and the Solicitor General (possibly Serjeant Welsh under a General Retainer for the Chamber, acting in the name of the Solicitor General at the Hearing) Counsel for the Chamber both perhaps having returned to their London Chambers, the Agreement has all the markings for Follett and Coleridge creating "the Deal" for an immediate resolution of the Case. To be borne in mind, William Webb Follett was a Topsham man, by right of birth, *(even if not born in the House in Ferry Road Topsham with its plaque indicating that he was – strong evidence suggests that he was actually born elsewhere in Topsham).*

As a result of these negotiations, Robert Davy agreed to supply the Limestone for the new Lock and the Chamber agreed to fashion and pay for its construction, in place of the original Lower Sluice. The Works were completed in 1832, having complied with the terms of the Canal Extension Act 1829. The full terms of the Agreement in both transcribed and facsimile form will follow at the ending of this Chapter.

It is interesting to note the very last-minute amendments and additions, inserted in the hand of Hugh Myddelton Ellicombe, the City Chamberlain and Attorney, who attended and witnessed the signing of the Agreement on the 26th March 1829. This meant that "negotiations" were ongoing to the very table of the Signing and Completion, with no time for "re-engrossing" the document in its final version by the Chamber's Scrivener, the Engrossing Clerk on his High Stool. *("Bartleby the Scrivener"* – Herman Melville*)* so unlike the word-processor of later times.

From my own memory of lost times, these last-minute adjustments happen at the very Meeting itself, when the Parties, with some solemnity and formality, if not pomp, meet in order to "Sign, Seal and Deliver" the Agreement, in duplicate. The City Archives includes the original Part of the Agreement signed by Robert Davy and witnessed by H M Ellicombe himself and one other. This speed of action well explains the pressure and anxiety on the part of the Chamber to reach completion, with its Parliamentary Bill for the Canal Extension already having been authorised to be solicited in London by H M Ellicombe together with *"such Members of the Chamber… as he may think most advantageous for the interests of the Chamber"* (n.b. not the "City".) - Minute of the Navigation Committee dated 9th *February 1829).*

To date, the Working Drawings of Topsham Lock by James Green have not been traced, but the speed of progress suggests that they might have been readily to hand. A Minute of the Navigation Committee dated 7th October 1828 states *"Mr Green having laid before this Committee a Plan of the proposed lock opposite Topsham which is approved: Ordered that he do prepare a Report of the best method of carrying the Plan into effect to be laid before the next Chamber."*

It was at the very last minute that the obligations upon the Chamber under this Agreement were included in the Canal Extension Bill, which was enacted on the 14th May 1829 *(George IV – Cap. xlvii)*. It is straightforward to identify these last "eleventh-hour" amendments to include the Topsham Lock, even if the Parliamentary Draftsman's Pen did not include it in the Act's Title, which is just *"An Act for altering, extending and improving the Exeter Canal"* - a little rich for using language relating to *future intended* Works rather than retrospectively "Approving & Endorsing" Works already long completed.

In the light of the time now being taken to obtain any Parliamentary approval to anything, the sheer expedition given to these local events must be noted, having regard to all the other pressures upon Parliamentary time, when realising the context of all other matters of national importance going on in the background. (Chapter Two and Appendix 1). The Chamber's Bill was laid before Parliament, following the Chamber affixing its Common Seal to the final draft, as recommended by the Navigation Committee under its Minute of the 9th February 1829, being destined for imminent enactment, it was so soon after, on the **11th February 1829** that the Court Case for the Mandamus received its Hearing, followed by the Agreement between Robert Davy and the Chamber on the **26th March 1829** (just 6 weeks after the Hearing), and then by the Canal Extension Act being passed and enacted on the **14th May 1829** (only 7 weeks later than the Agreement).

Also, to be carefully noted, under Chapter III of the Exeter Canal Extension Act 1829, it was expressly provided that Topsham Lock *"shall at all Times ever hereafter be maintained and kept in good Repair and Condition by the said Mayor, Bailiffs and Commonalty, and that etc etc…"* after the Lock had been completed, on the terms defined in the Act.

Topsham Lock (sometimes termed the "Side Lock" to the Canal) is 91ft in length, inside lock, 25ft 6in wide, outside lower gate, 24 ft. 3¼ in. In the Spring of 1976 this statutory access from the Canal to the Exe through Topsham Lock was "stanked" (i.e. staked) off for structural reasons following a Survey, and it so remains in disuse. The Exeter Port Authority is now seeking to re-invigorate the commercial usage and profitability of the Canal, with consequent legal implications arising under the 1829 Act, if Topsham Lock is left remaining in disuse and in an increasing state of decay and abandonment.

The Agreement dated 26th March 1829, entered into by Robert Davy with the Mayor Bailiffs and Commonalty of the City of Exeter is now set out, together with the facsimile of the original Agreement included in addition.

"**Dated 26 March 1829**

Mr Robert Davy with the Mayor Bailiffs and Commonalty of the City of Exeter **Agreement**

Articles of Agreement entered into this Twenty sixth day of March in the year of our Lord One thousand eight hundred and twenty-nine. **Between Robert Davy** of Wear in the Parish of Topsham in the County of Devon Timber and Coal Merchant for himself his Executors and Administrators of the one part and **The Mayor Bailiffs and Commonalty of the City of Exeter** of the other part **Whereas** the said Mayor Bailiffs and Commonalty have applied for and are now soliciting an Act of Parliament for altering extending and improving the Exeter Canal **And Whereas** it has been lately proposed and it is now fully meant and intended between the said parties that in lieu of the late Entrance at Lower Sluice there shall be a Clause introduced in such Bill for the purpose of securing the Erection of a Lock Entrance into the said Canal to be placed above the Town of Topsham in lieu of the Entrance at the late Lower Sluice such newly intended Lock Entrance to be placed in such convenient and proper place near to Stone Gutter as may be best effected and made capable of passing all such Vessels as could have heretofore passed at any time up the old Canal and that the Expence of the formation of such Lock and Entrance shall be borne and paid by the said Mayor Bailiffs and Commonalty of Exeter and that all Vessels entering such newly intended Lock and all goods passing through the same shall be charged with the same Tonnage and Tolls as if such vessels or Goods had passed the Entrance of the said Canal at Turf **And Whereas** previous to the said arrangement it was proposed that an Agreement in writing should be entered into by the said Robert Davy to supply and deliver or cause to be supplied and delivered free of all Expences to the said Mayor Bailiffs and Commonalty except as hereafter mentioned in aid of and towards the Costs of such Lock Entrance All the Lime Stone which shall be required and found necessary for the building of such Lock and for depositing such Lime Stone as near as depth of water will permit the depth to come at some convenient place for the conveniently carrying on and completing the works of such intended new Lock Entrance as aforesaid stood **Now these Presents Witness** and He the said Robert Davy doth hereby covenant and agree with the said Mayor Bailiffs and Commonalty and their successors That in the Event of the aforesaid proposed Act passing into a Law and the same containing such Provisions and Clauses therein as deemed necessary and proper and shall be effectual to provide for the restoration of an Entrance above the Town of Topsham by the Erection of a Lock as aforesaid by and at the Expence of the said Mayor Bailiffs and Commonalty and for their commencing the building of such Lock and proceeding therewith according to the true meaning and intentions of such Act then He the said Robert Davy his Executors or Administrators shall and will within one Month from and after the passing of such Act if required so to by the said Mayor Bailiffs and Commonalty on

The Agreement dated 26th March 1829 -- Robert Davy & the Chamber

their Agent in that behalf begin to supply and continue to provide and find at his and their own proper Costs and Charges all such Lime Stone and of such good and sufficient Quality and Quantity as shall be necessary and proper and be required for the building erecting and completing such Lock Entrance as aforesaid (so that the Stone required as aforesaid be not larger or of greater weight than the said Robert Davy is enabled to ship or unship without the aid of Machinery and if any Stone of greater weight or magnitude shall be required than he can procure without the use of machinery that then and in such case the said Mayor Bailiffs and Commonalty shall find and provide the Cranes or Machinery and also pay a moiety of the labor necessary for the purpose of shipping and unshipping any Stones of such greater weight or magnitude) the future repairs of the said Lock Entrance being done by and the Expence of the said Mayor Bailiffs and Commonalty And also shall and will at his own like Costs and Charges deliver such Lime Stone or cause the same to be delivered at and upon some place near adjoining the Site of such intended Lock such place to be determined on by the Engineer employed in the erecting or superintending the Erection of such Lock and there deposit the same for the convenience of commencing the building and carrying on and completing such intended Lock according *(to)* the true Intent and Meaning of the parties hereto being for the purpose of securing the Erection of a proper and efficient Lock Entrance from the Tideway of the River Exe above the Town of Topsham near to the said place called Stone Gutter or at such other place as may hereafter be fixed not more than two hundred and sixty yards of three feet to the yard above the Bridge across the Canal opposite to Topsham Ferry so as to communicate with the said Canal and being capable of conveying and passing all such Ships and Vessels as could have heretofore passed the old Canal from the late Lower Sluice to Exeter anything contained or to be contained in the said Act as to the payments of the whole Costs and Expences of the said Lock Entrance by the said Mayor Bailiffs and Commonalty to the contrary hereof in any wise notwithstanding **In Witness** whereof I the said Robert Davy to these presents have hereto set my hand and seal the day and year first above written.

Signed, sealed and delivered by the said Robert Davy (signature of) Robert Davy, L.S. in the presence of: H M Ellicombe (He was the Chamberlain and City Attorney & Solicitor); H M Ford

Articles of Agreement entered into this twenty sixth day of March in the year of our Lord One thousand eight hundred and twenty nine *Between Robert Davy* of War Merchant for himself his Executors and administrators of the one part *and The Mayor Bailiffs and Commonalty* of the City of Exeter of the other part *Whereas* the said Mayor Bailiffs and Commonalty have applied for and are now soliciting an Act of Parliament for altering extending and improving the Exeter Canal *And Whereas* it has been lately proposed and it is now fully meant and intended between the said parties that in lieu of the late Entrance at Lower Sluice there shall be a Clause introduced in such Bill for the purpose of securing the Erection of a New Entrance into the said Canal to be placed above the Town of Topsham in lieu of the Entrance at the late Lower Sluice such newly intended Lock Entrance to be placed in such convenient and proper place near to Stone Gutter as may be best effected and made capable of passing all such Vessels as could have heretofore passed at any time up the old Canal and that the Expence of the formation of such Lock and Entrance shall be borne and paid by the said Mayor Bailiffs and Commonalty of Exeter and that all Vessels entering such newly intended Lock and all goods passing through the same shall be charged with the same Tonnage and Tolls as if such Vessels or Goods had passed the Entrance of the said Canal at Turf *And Whereas* previous to the said arrangement it was proposed that an agreement in writing should be entered into by the said Robert Davy to supply and deliver or cause to be supplied and delivered free of all Expence except as hereafter mentioned to the said Mayor Bailiffs and Commonalty in aid of and towards the Costs of such Lock Entrance All the Lime Stone which shall be required and found necessary for the building of such Lock and for depositing such Lime Stone as near as depth of Water will permit the depth to come at some convenient place for the conveniently carrying on and completing the works of such intended new Lock Entrance as aforesaid *Now these Presents Witness* and the the said Robert Davy doth hereby covenant and agree with the said Mayor Bailiffs and Commonalty and their Successors that in the Event of the aforesaid proposed Act passing into a Law and the same containing such Provisions and Clauses therein as deemed necessary and proper and shall be effectual to provide for the restoration of an Entrance above the Town of Topsham by the Erection of a Lock as aforesaid by and at the Expence of the said Mayor Bailiffs and Commonalty and for their commencing the building of such Lock and proceeding therewith according to the true meaning and intentions of such

270

Image of Agreement – Page 1.

The Agreement dated 26th March 1829 -- Robert Davy & the Chamber

Act then He the said Robert Davy his Executors or Administrators shall and will within one Month from and after the passing of such Act if required so to do by the said Mayor Bailiffs and Commonalty or their Agent in that behalf begin to supply and continue to provide and find at his and their own proper Costs and Charges all such Lime Stone and of such good and sufficient Quality and Quantity as shall be necessary and proper and be required for the building erecting and completing such Lock Entrance as aforesaid (so that the Stone required as aforesaid be not larger or of greater weight than the said Robert Davy is enabled to ship or unship without the aid of Machinery and if any Stone of greater weight or Magnitude shall be required than he can procure without the use of Machinery that then and in such case the said Mayor Bailiff and Commonalty shall find and provide the Cranes or Machinery and also pay a Moiety of the labor necessary for the purpose of shipping and unshipping any Stones of such greater weight or Magnitude) the future repairs of the said Lock Entrance being done by and at the Expense of the said Mayor Bailiffs and Commonalty) And also shall and will at his own like Costs and Charges deliver such Lime Stone or cause the same to be delivered at and upon some place near adjoining the Site of such intended Lock such place to be determined on by the Engineer employed in the erecting or superintending the Erection of such Lock and there deposit the same for the Convenience of commencing the building and carrying on and completing such intended Lock according the true Intent and Meaning of the parties hereto being for the purpose of securing the Erection of a proper and efficient Lock Entrance from the Sideway of the River Exe above the Town of Topsham near to the said place called Stone Gutter or at such other place as may hereafter be fixed not more than Two hundred

Image of Agreement – Page 2.

and Sixty yards of three feet to the yards above the Bridge across the Canal opposite to Topsham Ferry so as to communicate with the said Canal and being capable of conveying and passing all such Ships and Vessels as could have heretofore passed the Old Canal from the late Lower Sluice to Exeter any Thing contained or to be contained in the said Act as to the payments of the whole Costs and Expences of the said Lock Entrance by the said Mayor Bailiffs and Commonalty to the contrary hereof in any wise notwithstanding In Witness whereof I the said Robert Cary to these presents have hereunto set my hand and seal the day and year first above written

Signed sealed and delivered by the said Robert Davy in the presence of

Robt. Davy

Image of Agreement – Page 3.

CHAPTER NINE
Hubris & Nemesis

Upon completion of the Extension to Turf, a ceremonial first tour of the whole Canal was held on the 15th September 1827, as the declared Formal Opening Day, followed that evening by a Grand Dinner of celebration, held by the Navigation Committee at the *Royal Clarence Hotel* in Exeter.

This was later followed on the 29th September 1830 by a Grand Procession with Barges and a Band to mark the opening of the new Basin at Exeter Quay and then by another Grand Dinner in the evening, at *Congdon's Royal Subscription Rooms,* given by "some 200 of the principal inhabitants" to show the approval of the City, for the Mayor and the Exeter Chamber, at which the Mayor Robert Rogers Sanders rose to give his Reply for the Guests, as will be referred to later in this Chapter.

The financial result of this Extension to Turf was that instead of an initial estimate for the Works of some £45,391.13s.6½d. based on the Report by James Green to the Navigation Committee, for referral to the Chamber, on the 11th December 1826 (which would have been an acceptable figure under the Green First Report 1820 if fully pursued), the Chamber incurred debt liabilities in excess of £106,000, (rising to a suggested £120,000) during the course of which the Chamber had recourse to the wholly improper use of Charity monies of which they were the Trustees (being the two Charities known as the *Atwill's* and the *Awliscombe* Charities), to help fund the accrued debts arising from the Extension works.

Full reference was made to this improvidence in the 1834 Report of the Royal Commission for proposals to reform local government structures nationwide, under which the two appointed Commissioners for Exeter, Henry Roscoe and Edward Rushton, in their First Report dated 8th May 1834 (including a Section relating to "Topsham Quay and State of the River" as set out in Chapter Ten and Appendix 8) gave an excoriating review and critique of the flagrant breaches of general public accountability and wholesale mismanagement by the Chamber of the Canal Extension Works.

The unlawful misuse by the Chamber of Charity finances of which the Chamber were the Trustees was found inexcusable. This itself led to the Two Suits in Chancery being brought against the Chamber by the Charities in question, which were current, even if dormant, because the Members of the Chamber were the only judges as to the approval of Funds to press these Cases with rigour… *(a question of a conflict of interests?)*, whilst the Canal Extension Bill and the Davy Court case for a Mandamus were in progress.

The fate of the Chamber was overtaken by the Municipal Corporations Act 1835 (see Chapter One – Provenance and Chapter Ten and Appendix 8) which was of national importance for the reorganisation of all such local authorities. In Exeter, the Chamber was dissolved and replaced by a new Council, with no sanctions sought against its former Members for the consequences of their imprudent actions.

In the light of what was to follow in 1834 under the Commissioner's First Report as above, relating to the catastrophe of the whole Canal Extension venture and its crippling financial consequences, it is the truculent tone and "edge" of the public speech given on 29th September 1830 by the then Mayor, Mr Robert Rogers Sanders, Esq, in his Reply on behalf of the Guests at the Dinner that might suggest a degree of complacency, if not a touch of hypocrisy, on his part, in expressing such pride in the entire Canal Works, apart from the implied public "upbraiding" of Robert Davy and reference being made to when *"a hostile feeling arose in the neighbouring town of Topsham"*. In seeking the cheers of the Guests, with Robert Davy himself not being present, the speech deserves to be included in this Book in Appendix 6, for the Reader to adjudge.

In exercising the rights of Topsham traders under the law, it might well be said that Robert Davy could be honoured as a "Hero".

The challenge to the Chamber's position, for which Robert Rogers Sanders remained the unqualified apologist to the bitter end, is shown in the several letters published in the Western Times, from the Topsham inhabitants' perspective and they are included in Appendix 7, commencing on the 20th October 1827 after the Extension had been cut and before Robert Davy brought his Case in May 1828, then on the 24th May 1828 just when the Rule for Mandamus had been granted, then on 11th October 1828 and the 27th December 1828 when the Consent Order had been made for the Hearing in February 1829.

What these letters do indicate is the lack of any dialogue of understanding between the Chamber and the Town of Topsham, as to the Chamber's actions, including any evidence of thought having been given to having two Locks in the Extension plans in the first place, whether at the Lower Sluice or a little further down river, whilst at least recognising the common ground of all parties in their accepting the gravity of the problems with the Lower Sluice, which needed urgent attention, so quick had been the decision to press on to the new Lock at Turf Pool, with the commercial motivation of by-passing Topsham

Quay as a political spur for the future trading benefit of Exeter.

Much influence remained with Robert Rogers Sanders, whose family connections with the City were long established and extensive, apart from his own businesses, one of which, of the more "manufacturing" nature, trading in iron, hemp and tallow, as previously noted in Chapter Six, he had sold to one Robert Davy no less. The Chamber's Bankers were the Exeter Bank, which happened to be controlled by the Sanders family, of whom Robert Rogers Sanders was a prominent Member. In promoting the Canal Extension and dealing with the accruing Debts arising from its unforeseen excesses, it is thus likely that Robert Rogers Sanders might have had a "conflict of interests".

It was the same gentleman who told the Parliamentary Commissioners in 1833 that Exeter was the "Ever-Faithful City" which would not admit Dissenters to its Chamber, despite the removal of legal restrictions with the abolition of the Test Acts. I am wholly indebted to the fascinating work by Robert Newton in his book *"Eighteenth Century Exeter"* for this engaging background. Four of the Sanders family voted for the (unsuccessful) Tory candidate in the Parliamentary Election of December 1832. The Sanders family had been powerful Merchants in the 17th Century, emerging as epitomes of the rising Middle Class, albeit in "Trade". By the 18th Century they had "moved" upwards from Trade to become professional __men__ (note my deliberate use of the word "men") exemplified by Robert Rogers Sanders being a successful Wine Merchant, perhaps very slightly above the social ranks of Brewers such as William Crockett - although when the Canal Extension had been built, William Crockett insisted that the Ship carrying his 3 hogsheads of Gin which had docked at Topsham Quay, then had to go back downriver in order to access the Canal at Turf Lock, increasing the passage Toll for the Shipowner there by tenfold, the costs of the Gin being but a quarter of the shipping costs. He would not allow it to be transported into Exeter by land carriage from Topsham Quay at a much cheaper rate. (Pride and Principle over Common Sense...).

When you were elected a Member of the Chamber, you had "arrived" There were Doctors and Surgeons there, including Philip de la Garde, the ophthalmic surgeon, who had written that Memoir for the Institution of Civil Engineers upon the History of the Canal (see Chapter Four and the Reports of James Green in Appendix 3) and happened to be the City's last Mayor before the Chamber was put aside under the reforms of the Municipal Reform Act 1835.

Whilst the Members' personal characters are deemed beyond reproach and I do not seek to say or imply otherwise, (Topsham Lock is a problem for me of issues beyond personalities) their apparent sense of entitlement, self-assurance and superiority, if not quite epistemic insouciance, in looking after their own Class interests of both Church and State seem to have moved them away from their former ancestral roles in developing and maintaining the dynamic of the thriving industrial and commercial City which their forebears had helped forge.

They had lost that connection between their powers as the governing municipal authority and the population whom they were meant to represent and serve. The letters quoted to the Western Times speak very much on this division in a Society that had become "Them and Us". Sanders and Davy seem to represent this sad divide.

Further Extracts from the local Press of the time to this effect are included in Appendix 7, noting in particular the "Can of Worms" piece in the Western Times edition of the 20th January 1838 whilst in the "Exeter Canal Account" in the Western Times edition of the 28th October 1837 of the Meeting of the Council held on the **23rd October 1837**, there is substantiated the crucial element in my whole Argument, in which Meeting the Council Member Mark Kennaway gave a devastating critique and forensic analysis of the entire scandal, as he objected to any softening down of the <u>Report of the Committee of the whole Council upon the Canal Expenditure Account</u>, (which he had Chaired) which was then tabled by the Town Clerk and read as follows:

"It was resolved, that this Committee is unable to discover among the records of the late Chamber, any authority for the execution of a work involving the expenditure disclosed by Mr Crockett's account. Neither can they find any Order of the Chamber directing Mr Crockett to make the payments set forth in that account. That the accounts of the expenditure and vouchers for the payments are both so irregular, that it is difficult to say what is the most unsatisfactory. That the communication of the late chamber to this Council sets forth no reason for this large account (extending over a period of eight years) not having been examined and allowed by that Body. For these reasons the Committee considers that it will be the duty of the Council to record its refusal to allow the account."

Eventually, after fierce arguments and some "fine-tuning", with the first vote to Refuse the Account having been lost by a majority of only one (16 For – 17 Against) the Report was accepted by a majority, of only one (15 vs. 14).

In Member Mark Kennaways's masterly speech, one of total politeness and scrupulous courtesy as he addressed the issues and not the personalities, neither Messrs Crockett and Sanders were blessed with unbounded praise, with Mr Sanders' style being implied as condescending to the public at large if not arrogant, as he might be thought of as thinking *"that he considered the public have neither right to look at nor speak to that body"* (i.e. the Chamber) and then Mark Kennaway made the salient comment, (which supports my own Argument), that *"**I do not think that Mr Green would have acted as he did unless he had been aided or abetted by persons possessing undue influence ....**"*

Mr Kennaway's speech is much too lengthy and detailed to be included in this Chapter but some highly significant points must be mentioned. On the question of the Committee having been unable to find any authority from the Chamber for the Works, Mr Sanders' spokesman, Mr Drake, sought to argue that even if there was no <u>direct</u> authority, then there was *"plenty of <u>implied</u> authority"* and that he would say *"as to the Exeter Bank, and in fact to all that*

Mr Crockett did, he was virtually sanctioned by the body. I do not say that it was proper, for it was the most irregular proceeding that was ever adopted in a work of such magnitude."

Much debate resulted on this aspect, where the ice of justification was clearly very thin.... There was also debate as to the roles and relationships as between the Navigation Committee and the Chamber and who knew and did what, when. I have referred previously to my difficulty in always finding the lines of communication between these two bodies, accepting that Robert Rogers Sanders was a Member of both, having been appointed to the NC on the 18th April 1825, as well as being the Mayor in 1830.

Much detail was given about the lack of accounting by Mr Crockett, with the Exeter Bank lending monies on some seemingly erratic basis, including an order for an extra £10,000 to be borrowed in order to complete Topsham Lock, dated 10th March 1830.

James Green was ordered on the 9th March 1830 to make an estimate of the whole expense to complete the work and basin, with further monies of £13,000 ordered to be borrowed to complete the work with a letter to Exeter Bank to let Mr Crockett *"overdraw his account to the amount of £5,000"*. After this, a Committee was appointed on the 13th November 1830 to examine Mr Crockett's Accounts, but the Committee never met!! At this, the Mayor apparently said, to the opposite, *"The Committee met and directed that Bonds should be sealed to Messrs, Sanders for £2,800."*

Matters became a little fractious, with Mark Kennaway seeking to lower the temperature with phrases such as *"discussing this subject without any excitement discharged of all personal feeling, and looking at it dispassionately"* and *"It was certainly my object in drawing up this Report to free it from all asperity of expression"*.

He begged to say that there was no such thing as any indirect authority for the large payments set forth in Mr Crockett's Account, granted that there had been no direct authority to begin with. *"The main feature of my objection is – and where I think all the mischief has been effected, has been by Mr Crockett construing the authority to receive, and hold money, into an authority to pay and disburse – I maintain that is the root and source of all the evil."*

Mr Crockett had not drawn the distinction between the receiving of monies as Treasurer, and assuming the authority to pay out sums without any order.

There then followed a rather acrimonious exchange on the point that Robert Rogers Sanders had said that the people challenging this whole scenario were ignorant of what they were asserting because they had suffered *"from insufficient information"*. To the contrary, this Report detailed at length the full knowledge of the Works and the defects that had required remedy, based on the two remedies suggested by James Green (in his two Reports). The only point missed was that Mark Kennaway referred only to the second Option put by James Green of *"an extension of the canal to a point on the river, I believe*

Turf and all the advantages of these works, respectively were set forth, with all the disadvantages of the canal in its then condition" ... (n.b. in this belief, he missed the option in the First Green Report 1820 suggesting an extension just a little further down the river. It was the James Green Report 1824 that took the option all the way down to Turf Pool.) – see Chapter Four.

So, it was Robert Rogers Sanders who was wrong, whether and when he was both a Member of the NC (April 1825) and/or the Chamber, or not. His role in Exeter Bank, if then active, was not mentioned specifically but at least behind the scenes, as a strong and influential supporter of Mr Crockett, he must be credited with having an ear to the ground in all matters of the Canal Extension and its financing. His ignorance of events generally cannot be in doubt when Mark Kennaway makes the following crucial comments, which deserve my highlighting, namely – *"Here then I have another proof of the extent of Mr Sander's information, and the result of Mr Green's improvements. It was stated by Mr R R Sanders, through Mr Drake, who spoke for him, that our trade was going to decay, and our commerce was forsaking us – that Exmouth received a large share and Topsham was taking the residue of our trade, and that if we had not taken this step* (i.e. of extending the Canal down to Turf and by-passing Topsham) *the city would have been ruined."*

So, now we have it, clear as crystal – the mercantile and political decision to by-pass Topsham Quay. I rest my case. If the modest extension down river to Topsham had been implemented, as suggested in the James Green Report 1820, then of course Topsham would NOT have been so by-passed.

Mark Kennaway then challenged the statements made by Mr R R Sanders to the Committee preparing this Report under debate and which Mr R R Sanders had signed as then Chairman of the former Chamber, regarding both the finances and budgets for the Works as they proceeded, with the cross-over of powers and functions between the Navigation Committee and the Chamber and the role of James Green thereunder and also the financial returns gained or lost following the trade through the Extended Canal, because there was an attempt to assert benefits and increased profits from the Extension by the new usage of larger vessels when the reality was that the Charges for using the Canal from Turf had increased tenfold (no longer the 5s per vessel as under the Old Days of the Lower Sluice) and no account was being included as to the huge debts incurred and still outstanding with increasing cost when adding the accruing interest to be paid (*to the Exeter Bank in which Mr R R Sanders apparently had a family interest or influence*).

The debts now evidenced that the undertaking was actually indebted £140,000. Referring to the Creditors of the Works, Mark Kennaway reports that

"The creditor moreover is beginning to see how the matter stands, and says that his debt ought to be redeemed. He is now thinking whether he will not call upon you to redeem it out of any surplus after payment of interest when

> *there is any such, and if the creditor can do so, when does Mr R R Sanders, who says 'he shall always feel delight when he thinks on the share he had in this undertaking,' think it possible the city can ever again obtain one sixpence from that canal while before his work of delight paid clear £4,000 a year."*

There then followed a detailed challenge to the belief that the Extension Works had increased the Trade to Exeter with any new trade beyond what the wants of the inhabitants required.

> *"As for what Mr R R Sanders says of the South American trade – without meaning anything offensive, I shall merely say that there is a word in very common use which would aptly describe that assertion."*

[I could not possibly offer any comment on what such a word might be and if it were the same then, as now]. Whilst Mark Kennaway credited an empathic supporter of the catastrophe with having

> *"no other end or object in view than the benefit of the community, that I know you never expected any profit or ever had any, and I never thought otherwise. But I say that you misplaced your confidence, and that those gentlemen on whom you relied have not done you justice"…*

In showing that the aim of attracting the biggest ships into the Canal, by reason of the depth having been increased to draw a 12 ft depth throughout, had not been achieved, he continued that

> *"the trade now (1837) by the large class of vessels is comparatively nothing",* and that *"The large mass of trade is still carried on in the vessels under 100 tons"* If it was then stated that *"the Canal has made Exeter",* did it never occur to *"those gentlemen"* that *"Exeter had made the Canal?"*

Reference was then made to the letter sent to the Council by Mr R R Sanders with Mark Kennaway commenting on it that in Mr R R Sanders

> *"considering the state of the trade of the Port, the public had a right to look to the Chamber for improvement, this is rather a new doctrine from such a quarter, for I thought he (Mr R R Sanders) considered the public have neither right to look nor speak to that body, constituted as it was in his time.".* (Strong words indeed).

Then to repeat this very important piece of my Argument, he added
"I do not think that Mr Green would have acted as he did unless he had been aided or abetted by persons possessing undue influence" (i.e. Messrs Crockett and Sanders).

Another Councillor, Mr Snell, gave a full supporting statement for Mark

Kennaway, in regard to

> "*those curious productions (i.e. letters) of Mr Robert Rogers Sanders. There was a boldness, a recklessness of style about these letters, which any right-thinking man would shrink from, under the circumstances, and it was yet to be seen whether even this gentleman would not be made to quail before public opinion.*"

Mr Mark Kennaway received the cordial thanks of the Council for the manner in which he had brought up the Report, and for his temperate tone which had characterised his entire conduct, especially when accused of asperity in the process. Mr R R Sanders had stated

"there were those who feared, and others who wished its failure [i.e. the Canal Extension to Turf] – was it fair for Mr Sanders to insinuate this calumny? - it was easy for him to malign the characters, and asperse the motives of persons, whom he refrained from naming..."

Mr Kennaway said that 13 letters had been received from late Members of the Chamber and all of them, with the exception of Mr de la Garde, who thought the investigation "*inquisitorial*" excepted *(sic)* the point – they all excepted *(sic)* the expense, and the whole mystery was explained by this assumption of Mr Crockett, who said that he felt himself justified in paying, "*by virtue of his **corporate character**...*"

The Mayor then said that there had been no letter from himself but he felt it due to himself to state, as a member of the new body, and of the old, that he and those who acted with him, had constantly called on Mr Crockett for the production of his Account. He would say, again, that if the old Chamber thought they were going to lay open the whole treasures of the earth – they could [*not?*] have proceeded in a more profuse manner. (Hear, hear). It was accepted that the only question in mind was not whether Mr Crockett had misappropriated any funds but whether he had paid it properly or improperly.

With one agreed amendment of additional words being added, the Report was carried without division. The following is the Clause with the additional words in brackets,

> "*It was Resolved, that this Committee is unable to discover, among the Records of the late Chamber, any authority for the execution of a work involving the expenditure disclosed by Mr Crockett's account; neither can they find any Order of the Chamber directing Mr Crockett to make [a large proportion of] the payments set forth in that Account: and thus altered, it was passed unanimously.*

As a footnote to this important Meeting, a Motion was laid for Mr Crockett to repay to the City the sum of £166.9s.0d, being the amount of interest accrued on two Accounts which he had charged for the Beer which his own Brewery had supplied, as a separate private business matter, albeit raised on the Chamber's accounts connected with the Canal Extension, in respect of sustenance for the navigators employed on the Works. Mr Crockett's lawyer assured the Chamber *"that Mr Crockett was safe for £166-9s-0d"* which was not doubted by the Chamber but which thought *"the money might as well be fructifying for the use of the City as in Mr Crockett's hands."*

At this point of the Book, it does seem that what had been a matter of conflicting issues and interests over mercantile affairs has also highlighted the personalities of the three major participants involved in the saga of Topsham Lock. Of Robert Davy, there emerges the story of a powerful Topsham Trader and Businessman who was not overtaken by the need for social status or the airs and graces of a gentleman in "polite Society", but of a man robust and vigorous in defence of his own perceived interests which embraced his own affairs as well as those of the Topsham community. It might be thought that he could be stubborn in holding to his decisions and that his dealings with "Authority" suggests that he could prove "difficult". As an example, as evidenced in the NC Minutes previously cited in Chapter Six, he always refused to pay Town Dues upon goods landed at his Countess Wear wharfs (for whatever reason).

In contrast stand the gentlemanly "firm" of "Crockett & Sanders", whose combination of names is as worthy of the Attorney's Brass Plate on his High Street Offices as that, say, of "Wilson, Keppel & Betty"! The power and influence of these men held sway over the Chamber in Exeter. Their actions for promoting the Canal Extension were sustained by their conviction that it was the "right thing to do", in the best interests of the Chamber. They were simply being true to their own convictions. What they believed was the right thing to do, they implemented, both being men not crippled by their own modesty. This explains why there was no murmur or suggestion of them misappropriating or diverting any of the Chamber's Funds for their own personal uses or advantage. I am anxious to exclude any such innuendoes from my Argument for this Book.

After reading Mark Kennaway's Report and the extracts of the Council's Meeting at which he defended its conclusions, surprise cannot be avoided in how Mr Crockett the Brewer could have ever owned and managed a Brewery, albeit using his own private monies, when his lack of proper (or any) accounting principles and common prudence when handling public finances, was evidenced and recorded as such incompetence beyond belief. The impious thought arises of a Bungling Brewer who could not even organise a "little drinks party" in his own Brewery.

In contrast, the figure of Mr Robert Rogers Sanders emerges as a Silver-Smooth Operator, a man well geared to being "on public manoeuvres", who was well aware and accustomed to exercising his privileged authority in the public marketplace. For him, the right thing to do was what he believed should be done, with the confidence and self-assurance granted to those who "Never

Apologise, Never Explain". This position he applied equally to the public finances as well, likely, as his own. To repeat, no personal dishonesty is being suggested or implied. Events regarding Topsham Lock and Canal Extension were to prove him wrong in both judgments and actions, even if forever upheld by him within the rigid ethic of his own personal integrity.

As between these two commanding figures, might there be glimpsed, just in between the narrowest of social cracks, that the one was a Brewer – the other, a Wine Merchant?

These thoughts are my Fragments, held solely within my own personal sense of the story. There might well be other more contrasting or opposing perspectives but, in terms of the history of Topsham Lock, I will hold to my Argument as developed in this Book, upon the issues that it seeks to explore and understand.

CHAPTER TEN

The Commissioners' Report on Exeter and the Chamber 1834

The Municipal Corporations Act 1835 *(5 & 6 Will 4 c.76)*, sometimes known as the Municipal Reform Act was the Act that fundamentally reformed local Government in the Incorporated Boroughs of England and Wales. It stems from the social upheavals of the changes in England, as canvassed in Chapter Two and in Appendix 1, when a rural society with its Agricultural Revolution was fast changing into an urban society with its Industrial Revolution.

Central to this fluid scene came the Great Reform Act of 1832, which brought the first shoots of a wider Parliamentary democracy into the Country, with its wider franchise. For those of us from decades ago who remember the Schoolroom, with its Desks, Blackboard, Chalk & Scratchy Rubbing-out Block, and Inkwells (with the Ink Monitor) when History was taught in linear fashion, we usually began with "the Tudors", skirmished "the Stuarts" and the Civil War, until "the *(sic)* Glorious Revolution of 1688," then passed quickly through "the Georges" and eventually arrived at "the Victorians." Here we reached the Rotten Boroughs of England – and who **cannot** remember "Old Sarum" being engraved on their memory for ever, as the classic example of the rottenest of the Rotten?

Changes had to come and in 1833 there began a form of quasi-Second-Doomsday exercise whereby it was realised that no one knew about how the Country was organised and governed, by whom and for whom. Everything was becoming outdated as Cities sprung up from villages, populations were fast increasing, and the Enclosures were decimating the Countryfolk numbers.

The main conclusions of this nationwide exercise included some very revealing states of current management. Corporations were exclusive bodies with no community of interest with the Town after which they were named. Some electorates were kept as small as possible. Some were mere "political engines" to maintain a particular party in its ascendancy. Members usually served for life

Old Sarum

and the corporate body was a self-perpetuating body. Roman Catholics and Dissenters, although no longer disabled from being Members (following the Repeal of the Test Acts) were systemically excluded (Mr R R Sanders in his evidence to the Commissioners). Vacancies were few and the best qualified not elected to fill the gaps.

Some, including Exeter, operated in almost total secrecy and local inhabitants could not obtain information on their operations without bringing expensive Law Suits (Mr R R Sanders in his reported remarks referred to in Chapter Nine). The gift of Freedom of the City lay with the Corporation and so were often political appointments. Often Juries in Court Cases were exclusively made up of Freemen. In some places (including Exeter) public funds had been expended on public works without adequate supervision, and large avoidable debts had accrued. This often arose from contracts being given to members of the Corporation or their friends or relations.

Municipal property was also treated as if it were only for the use of the Corporation and not the general population. [Does not this last part touch upon the Canal Extension and the by-passing of Topsham? It might touch on why the Contract did not go out to public tender, and why not also the supply of the beer for the navigators by possibly someone other than William Crockett with his Brewery ....?]

The Commission concluded its Report by stating that:

> "... the existing Municipal Corporations of England and Wales neither possess nor deserve the confidence or respect of Your Majesty's subjects, and that a

thorough reform must be elected, before they can become, what we humbly submit to Your Majesty they ought to be, useful and efficient instruments of local government."

The 1835 Act established a uniform system of municipal boroughs, to be governed by Town Councils elected by ratepayers. The reformed boroughs were obliged to publish their financial accounts and were liable to audit.

The Parliamentary Committee charged with overseeing this restructuring did not believe that they had sufficient powers to carry out a full review of the existing and outdated system. So, they recommended the appointment of a Royal Commission, with the country being divided into districts with Commissioners responsible for enquiring into Boroughs in each District.

So, the Government sent out Inspectors to each part of the Country (some 285 Towns) to establish the facts about each place and area, to enable a whole new structure of Local Government to be established, of a national and uniform nature. For Exeter, there came Two Commissioners, as part of the Report – Part 1 for the Midland, Western and South-Western Circuits. The two South Western Commissioners were Henry Roscoe and Edward Rushton and they delivered their Report on the City of Exeter on the 8th May 1834.

They also delivered an Appendix to the First Report, containing Sections including Topsham Quay and State of the River. These are of sufficient interest for Extracts to be included in this Chapter, whilst, in Appendix 8, there is also an Extract of an abridged Version of the Reports prepared by a Barrister and published in 1835.

Appendix to the First Report of the Commissioners appointed to inquire into THE MUNICIPAL CORPORATIONS IN ENGLAND AND WALES. Part 1, Midland, Western, and South-Western Circuits.

Reports from Commissioners - Exeter p.493, 1835

CITY OF EXETER. - Topsham Quay and State of the River.

REPORTS FROM COMMISSIONERS ON MUNICIPAL CORPORATIONS IN ENGLAND AND WALES.

The Canal Dues are levied under an Act of Parliament passed in the year 1829, entitled, "An Act for altering, extending and improving the Exeter Canal."

The Quay Dues are levied at Topsham on all goods landed at Topsham quay; they are collected according to an ancient table. The corporation purchased these dues from the Northmore family. Several complaints were made by merchants at Topsham respecting the condition of the quays at that port, which do not appear to have been kept in a proper state; and also, on the subject of the passage to the town of Topsham being impeded, in consequence of the negligence of the corporation in cleansing the harbour: both these points will be noticed in a subsequent part of this report.

Freemen are exempt from Town Dues. The corporation claim the right to levy these dues under the grant of the fee-farm which they have from Edward the 3rd: the duties are the same on articles imported from foreign ports and coast-ways. The corporation levy the town's dues on all goods imported into the port of Exeter, and they contend, that the limits of the custom-house port are the limits over which they have a right to collect the dues. These limits include Axemouth on the east and Teignmouth on the west, and all places between the two ports last mentioned. The payment of these dues had been frequently refused both at Topsham and in Exeter. The corporation, alleging that they cleansed the stream, have in all cases contested from Topsham and in Exeter succeeded in enforcing their right to the dues. The inhabitants of Teignmouth contend, that even admitting the right of the corporation to levy these dues at Topsham and in Exeter by virtue of the grant of Edw. the 3rd, such right cannot extend to Teignmouth, which is not part of the duchy, and that the grant of Edw. the 3rd was only a grant of such portion of the water as belonged to the duchy. In support of their view of the case, they referred to an account of an inquisition taken at Exeter in the year 1290, in the reign of Edw. the 1st, which is printed in a work written by a former chamberlain of the city; by which it appears, that the King at that time had the river and the whole course thereof, in right of the city of Exeter ; that is to say, from the Checkstone unto the bridge of the said city, called Exbridge; and the inhabitants of Teignmouth contend, that the right to levy dues is limited to the waters which were the King's in right of the city, and no further, and that the dues taken on the Exe are in consideration of the cleansing of the harbour. At Teignmouth and other places, out of the ancient port of Exeter, but within the custom-house port of that city, the corporation do not repair the harbours, or give any consideration for the dues which they levy.

The chamberlain of the corporation stated, in reply to our inquiry into this subject, that the question of the town's dues taken at Teignmouth involved a question of title, which had lately been much agitated, and the corporation, therefore, declined to enter into any explanation of their right to levy the dues, except merely stating, that the dues had been constantly levied as far back as the time of Elizabeth.

Reports from Commissioners - Exeter p.495, 1835

CITY OF EXETER. - Topsham Quay and State of the River.

REPORTS FROM COMMISSIONERS ON MUNICIPAL CORPORATIONS IN ENGLAND AND WALES.

The corporation are deeply in Debt. In the time of William 3rd, the sum of £6,000 was borrowed for the purpose of repairing the canal. From time to time the debt has been increased; and the corporation have also applied funds belonging to the charities, for which they were trustees, to various purposes of their own. The debt of the corporation now amounts to a very large sum, the principal part of which was incurred in extending and altering the Exeter Canal. Much difference of opinion was expressed respecting the propriety of the alteration.

The works at the canal were not constructed by public contract, and the enormous expenditure on the improvement of the canal was the subject of much complaint on the part of some of the merchants of the city. It appears that the corporation, when they embarked in this work at first, only contemplated repairing the old canal; but they afterwards resolved on considerably extending the work. On the old canal the passage of vessels was frequently delayed for want of water, and no vessel drawing more than nine feet could conveniently approach the city. The canal has doubtless materially increased the facility of vessels reaching the city, and it has enabled vessels of a greater draught to enter the port at dead neap tides. In consequence of the alteration the tolls have been materially increased upon many articles, and the charges bear a large proportion to the freight; sometimes as much as a fourth part of the freight on a coasting voyage. Whatever difference of opinion may exist as to the expediency of the alteration, there can be but one opinion as to the manner in which the work has been carried into execution. In the year 1819 an engineer was desired to survey the works for the purpose of repairing and improving them; and in consequence of a report then made by him, considerable alterations were made, and the locks, gates, &c. were put into complete repair. In 1824 the engineer made a further report, and recommended, for various reasons, the extension of the canal to a place called Turf, one mile and seven furlongs lower down the river than the lower sluices of the then existing canal. This report was submitted to Mr. Telford, and was confirmed by him. In May 1825 the work was commenced; but it does not appear that the corporation had either estimate or contract for the work done in 1824; nor was any estimate given for the work commenced in 1825 until the following year, when a further report, with an estimate for completing the canal with the bridge and basin, amounting to £45,391, was delivered. In the year 1831 it was stated, that the further sum of £10,921 would be requisite to complete the canal without the bridge. This sum was supplied, and the corporation, without obtaining a further estimate, and without the precaution of having the work executed by public contracts, proceeded to supply the further funds demanded from them for this work, until they had expended on the works alone £95,500 together with land purchased for the quay, £5,400, and the incidental charges, £5,627, amounting in all to £106,527. Under the new Act for making these alterations the tolls have been much increased. The old canal at the lower tolls yielded a revenue of rather more than £4,000 per annum. Before the late Act, vessels passing the canal paid a duty of 5s.6d. each, without reference to the burthen. Under the new Act, the corporation are empowered to levy 5s. on all vessels using the canal locks or basins under 10 tons burthen; 6d. per ton on all vessels above 10 tons and under 100 tons; and if the same be more than 110 tons, the sum of 9d. per ton.

Reports from Commissioners - Exeter p.496, 1835

CITY OF EXETER. - Topsham Quay and State of the River.

REPORTS FROM COMMISSIONERS ON MUNICIPAL CORPORATIONS IN ENGLAND AND WALES.

The inhabitants of Topsham complain that the corporation of Exeter take quay dues at Topsham and that they have not only not kept the quay at that place in good repair but that the inhabitants, who have been obliged to erect wharfs and quays in consequence of the neglect of the corporation in this respect, are notwithstanding compelled to pay quay dues to the corporation, though they do not use the corporation quay. The corporation have it in contemplation to erect a new crane and to repair the quay. A serious complaint also of the negligence of the corporation respecting the river was made to us. In all cases where the right to the town dues has been questioned, the corporation are stated to have alleged the cleansing of the harbour as a consideration. At present they certainly neglect to perform this important duty - a duty rendered much more serious, both with regard to the necessity as well as to the expense of its performance, since the new canal has been constructed. It was stated by pilots, and other competent persons, that before the new canal was constructed vessels drawing 13 feet water could be brought alongside the quay at Topsham at spring tides, and vessels drawing 10 feet at neap tides. The tides in the Exe are much affected by the wind, the extreme difference between spring and neap tides varying from five feet to seven feet. At the lowest neap tides, vessels drawing 10 feet could formerly be taken over the shoals and this could be done seven or eight years ago; but within the last eight years the depth of water at Topsham has decreased a foot and a half. Two years since, the steam-vessel The William the Fourth, drawing 10½ to 11 feet, could be brought to the wharf just below Topsham quay; but this cannot now be done, by reason of the water having decreased 1½ foot. The channel is filling up both in the sides and the centre. Since the embankment for the canal, which has enclosed a great space over which the tide formerly flowed, there is not nearly the same quantity of back-water; and probably some part of the evil has been occasioned by the confining of the water in the canal, which used to be let out by the lower sluice; the current was strong and contributed to keep the channel clear. The bottom of the river is mud and gravel, which might be removed by dredging. The attention of the corporation has been called to the state of the river. In December 1832, an application was made to the corporation respecting the choking of the channel, which application was not answered until May 1833, when it was said that it would be taken into consideration. The proprietors of steam-boats trading. between Topsham and London have expressed their willingness to meet the corporation in the way of contribution to the expense of cleansing the harbour. It may be conceived that the owners of vessels have a great interest in preserving the passage to the quay, when it is known that the expense of the voyage of a steam-boat, when she cannot approach the quay, is £8 greater than when she lands her cargo at the quay. If something be not speedily done the trade of Topsham will be very seriously injured; and the corporation will have to exact dues for quays which shipping cannot approach, and town's dues, in consideration of cleansing a port, one part of which is fast choking up. The engineer who constructed the canal denied that the embankment had anything to do with the obstructions in the navigation.

The Reports pull no punches and are excoriating in their criticism of the Chamber and its financial affairs, whilst they also show an empathy towards the Town of Topsham and its treatment and neglect of its Quay by the Chamber. With the arrival in 1835 of the new City Council under the revised structure of governance, it might be seen as a precursor of the fresh attitudes and approach to a new and more fulfilling relationship with the local population that brought forth and enabled the changes enacted in the Exeter Port Dues Act 1840. This will be explored next, in Chapter Eleven.

CHAPTER ELEVEN

The Exeter Port Dues Act 1840

By 1840 the Exeter City Council must have been coming to terms in its governance of the City with all the battle-weariness, stresses and strains under which they had laboured since their Canal Extension Works were planned in 1820, with the Green First Report 1820. Within that turbulent twenty-year span, Exeter had experienced the tectonic plates of their Society being ground together, each one of the several plates, whether national or parochial, set against the others in their various permutations.

Within this social, cultural, political, commercial and industrial maelstrom, the grit of the Great Reform Act 1832 was succeeded by the Municipal Corporations Act 1835, as the Chamber gave way to the Council amidst the continuing rumble of the public inquest into the financial scandal, despite the enactment of the Canal Extension Act 1829 having provided the statutory "cloak" for the Chamber's Members, as earlier detailed.

Following this intensive and expensive period for Exeter under both its Chamber and then its Council, it might well explain why the Port was not included under the provisions of the *Harbours, Docks and Piers Clauses Act 1847*. By 1847 the Council's financial resources were still very parlous, to be faced with yet another piece of Legislation to absorb, requiring corporate stamina and staff.

Having dealt in that 1829 Act with the equalisation of the **Tolls and Duties arising upon the Canal**, as between the new Topsham Lock and Turf Lock, the political climate was now ripe for the final part of a strategy in bringing all Port matters into harmony, by **equalising the Quay Dues** (formerly known as **Town Dues**), as between the two Quays of Exeter and Topsham, within the Port as now defined in the 1840 Act.

(noting the historic definition of those "Town Dues" which were excepted and preserved by the 1840 Act for goods landed within the limits of the historic wider and more extensive old Port, but for those now beyond the Cheek Stone Rock and thus being outside the newly defined Port – with

the Collection of such outside Town Dues being now in abeyance and abandonment by the Council, as confirmed to me on enquiry of the City Treasurer for this Book).

To be clear, under the 1840 Act those Town Dues formerly charged under the Exeter Quay Dues Collections were abolished (but only in respect of the Exeter Port jurisdiction as newly defined in the 1840 Act) and were substituted by the same Quay Dues as were then equalised with the Topsham Quay Dues, with all future Quay Dues to be the same for both Quays, as set out and to be charged and collected by reference to the lengthy Schedule in the 1840 Act.

To recall the admonitions of Lord Tenterden in the Davy Case, that he was willing to listen to the two Junior Counsel if they refrained from repetition, I will refer back to Chapter One with which I began this Book, as to the structure and rationale for the Exeter Port Dues Act to be enacted, with its role for the Topsham River Commissioners to be established thereunder.

On the 16th November 1839, the London Gazette published a Notice headed "Exeter Port Dues" that Application was to be made to Parliament in the ensuing Session for leave to bring in a Bill

"for altering, equalising, and defining the ancient dues, duties, or petty customs, commonly called Town Custom, Town Duty, and Town Dues, now levied and collected, or authorised to be levied and collected, by Charter or otherwise"…"and also to alter, vary, amend, and enlarge the powers and provisions of an Act, passed in the Thirty-first Year of the Reign of His Majesty, King Henry the Eighth, intitled "An Act for, … etc" Dated this Seventh day of November 1839. John Gidley, Town Clerk.

In the light of all recent events, it would seem that this Bill would prove of a non-contentious nature, and would generate neither heat nor dust in its journey through both Houses of Parliament, as recent past and unquiet matters were settling down. I now find a logic to accepting its aims and purposes, which also, through the writing of this Book, provides answers to my very first questions when being inducted into my duties as Clerk to the TRCs, namely: "How and why did the 1840 Act come into enactment? What had gone on before? What was its context?" Out of the innocence of ignorance but still blessed (or cursed) with an unbounded curiosity, there has slowly emerged a pattern, - the "shape of things" – even if still only in the Fragments as declared in my Introduction.

Events now took the strangest of turns, in May 1840, when there came "An Extraordinary Manoeuvre". The Bill had all but passed the Committee stage of the House of Commons when a Freeman of Exeter, who chanced to be there on other business, discovered that the Bill contained a Clause which would have made all Freemen liable to the payment of Town Dues, despite their long enjoyed right of Exemption, which had been especially preserved by the Reform Act 1832. The insertion of this unexpected Clause was against the recorded opinion of the Exeter City Council, and apparently was not in the draft of the Bill when it left Exeter *(The Minutes of the Navigation Committee are not of help to so confirm)*. The preamble to the Bill was clear that the Freemen's privileges were untouched. Was this an attempt to perpetuate an intentional fraud?

A petition to expunge the Clause was despatched at once. In the event the rights of the Freemen were preserved in the Bill and its subsequent enactment in the 1840 Act. The Clause to achieve this Confirmation of the Exemption was introduced into the Bill on the proposal of Sir John Buller, and "zealously supported" by **Sir William Follett**, Mr Divett, and the Members for Devon.

The story behind this story appears to be, as understood by most Members of the Council, including the Chairman of the Navigation Committee, that the Bill, as originally drafted by the Port Dues Committee in Exeter, protected the rights of the Freemen. These gentlemen in Exeter had successfully opposed an attempt to introduce a Clause which would deprive Freemen of their privileges. It was curious, then, that the Town Clerk, when asked in the Committee Room of the House of Commons what, in his opinion, would be the effect of the Bill, *as produced by him,* if it became the law of the land, acknowledged that it would take from the Freemen the right of exemption from Town Dues.

One of the **Liberal** Aldermen also, in the presence of another **Liberal** Alderman, who formed part of the Exeter delegation sent to London, said *"And, to speak the truth, it was our **intention** to do so."* This intention was considered an act of injustice towards the Freemen - an attempt to destroy those privileges enjoyed by them, as being property rights guaranteed by the Reform Act 1832. The Preamble to the Bill was quite clear in its wording to protect them. If these rights were destroyed this would amount to a partial repeal of the Reform Act itself. The Amendment to restore and entrench the rights of the Freemen was carried by 72 in favour, with 47 against. Amongst the "Ayes" were **the Hon. J Y Scarlett** , with **Sir W Follett** as one of the Tellers.

The Breviate of the amended Bill can be summarised, very briefly, thus: -

Town Dues: -
The petty customs called the Town Dues were to cease, for the newly defined statutory Port of Exeter, except for any cargoes, goods, wares or merchandize brought or imported in to any place outside the Port limit, at the Exmouth Entrance from the sea, marked by the Cheek Stone Rock. The Port of Exeter, as newly defined, was to charge and raise Quay Dues (*tolls, duties and sums of money*) according to the comprehensive List of items set out in the Schedule to the Act, at the same rates for both Quays at Exeter and at Topsham.

The restrictions on altering tolls under the Municipal Corporations Act 1835: -
These were removed and changed so that any reduction of tolls authorised by the 1840 Act was only to be with the consent of the Lords of the Treasury, subject to prior public notice being given.

Limits of the Port: -
A Clause defining the limits of the Port and that providing that vessels delivering their cargoes in any part of the river should be liable to the duties mentioned in the Schedule was struck out. A Clause was inserted to exclude the Act from extending beyond the River Entrance, commencing from the Cheekstone Rock.

Recovery of Tolls: -
Clauses for the payment of tolls and their recovery, in respect of those Tolls not to be abolished by the Act, not to be affected by the Act for the remedies for their recovery and the right to dispute them.

Application of Tolls: -
All tolls to be paid to the Borough Treasurer and paid into the Borough's Fund, except for the TRCs being paid such sum not exceeding £200, as might be equivalent to £25 per cent. of the net amount of tolls on goods landed in the Parish of Topsham and parts of the river connected with the Parish. The TRCs were empowered to borrow £500 on the credit of this payment *[this was to fund the duties of the TRCs for the annual costs of dredging the Topsham Channel and Topsham Quay etc]*

The Commissioners: -
This sets out those matters covered in Chapter One – the TRCs Provenance – and does not require repetition.

Protection of Navigation: -
This Clause has also been covered in Chapter One. A Clause empowering the Corporation to dig up wharfs, etc on the river and imposing a penalty of £100 on parties erecting such wharfs, etc. was struck out of the amended Bill.

Bye Laws: -
Clauses empowering the Corporation to make bye laws had been struck out.

Penalties: -
Amended Clauses were inserted for the recovery and application of penalties.

Freemen: -
The right of Exemption from Toll of the Freemen of the City is saved to them.

Savings: -
Clauses had been inserted for saving the rights of the Lords of the Manors of Exminster, Kenton, and Powderham, and those of the Lord Rolle, and of the devisees of Sir Francis Henry Drake and those of Sir Lawrence Vaughan Palk.

The Enactment of the 1840 Act on the 2nd June 1840 marks the end of a long and complicated saga and its timeline brings the purpose of this Book to an end.

Final "snippets" are that on the 23rd January 1840, the *Exeter Flying Post* reported of the Exeter Canal that

> "*We learn with great pleasure that there was no less a number than five hundred and eighty-three vessels and craft that passed in an out of the New Canal Lock, opposite the town of Topsham, during the past year*".

Finally, on the 28th January 1843, Mr Gidley, Town Clerk, Exeter, published a notice under the heading "Exeter Canal and Town Dues – TO BE LET BY AUCTION" that the Council were seeking to let for a Term of Three Years from Lady-day, 1843, the TOLLS and DUTIES arising upon the EXETER CANAL and also the EXETER TOWN DUES, now collected by the Council of Exeter, and their Officers, under the authority of **two several Acts of Parliament;** (*i.e.* the Canal Extension Act 1829 and the Exeter Port Dues Act 1840); also the… *(other properties of the Council at Exeter Quay)* … and the Profits of Towing Vessels to and from the Entrance Lock, at Turf, with Offices and Buildings, the whole producing an income of very large annual amount".

[This Farming out of the Revenue streams was a typical form of outsourcing by a Local Authority to bring in a fixed income, whether with or without a Capital premium for the start – which in Exeter's Case might have relevance to the debts arising from the Canal Extension venture and the concerns of Creditors. The Receivership of the Canal Business followed later as has been carefully explained by Mr Clew in his comprehensive history of "*The Exeter Canal*"].

AN ACT

FOR

Equalizing, defining and regulating the Petty Customs, and for facilitating the Collection thereof and of the Quay Dues payable to the Mayor, Aldermen and Burgesses of the City and Borough of *Exeter*, and for preserving the Navigation of the River *Exe*.

WHEREAS the Mayor, Aldermen and Burgesses of the city and borough of Exeter are seized of, and entitled to certain petty customs, duties or sums of money commonly called the Town Dues, payable in respect of certain goods, wares and merchandizes (being the property of persons not free of the said city of Exeter, or otherwise legally exempted from the payment thereof) imported into the port of Exeter, or certain parts thereof, from foreign parts beyond the seas, and imported or brought to the said port of Exeter, or certain parts thereof, coastwise or along the coasts of Great Britain:

(17.)   A   And

Exeter Port Dues Act - First page

CHAPTER TWELVE

The Interlink between (a) the Events of the Canal Extension Act 1829 & Topsham Lock and (b) the Events precipitating the 1840 Act

At this point it might be helpful to draw the scenario of there being two separate issues or "Battles" as between the townsfolk and traders of Topsham based at Topsham Quay on the one hand and the Chamber and the traders of Exeter based at Exeter Quay on the other.

There is an interval of 11 years between the two Acts, with the first in a material sense foreshadowing and leading to the second. Whilst each stood on its own, there can be no doubt that the latter was a consequence of the former.

First, the **construction of Topsham Lock by** 1832, as ordained under the **Canal Extension Act 1829** and following its last-minute incorporation within the Bill, as a result of the Agreement of 26th March 1829 which was reached immediately after the Davy Court Case judgment on the 11th February 1829.

Secondly, the **navigation of the Topsham channel** and the appointment of the Topsham River Commissioners under the **Exeter Port Dues Act 1840,** as a result of the dredging of the navigable channel at Topsham having been neglected by the Chamber, which had led to complaints being lodged with and heard by the two Commissioners, Henry Roscoe & Edward Rushton, appointed for (inter alia) reporting upon the Exeter Chamber, under the 1834 Commission enquiring into the Municipal Corporations in England and Wales. (See Chapter Ten and Appendix 8)

Until the enactment of the 1840 Act the management of both River and Canal were under the control of the Navigation Committee of the City of Exeter, a Committee created by the Chamber in 1814, acting within the aegis of the River Exe Act 1539.

It was following the 1840 Act that responsibility for dredging the Topsham channel (as defined within the Jurisdiction ordained in the 1840 Act) was transferred to the newly appointed/elected Topsham River Commissioners,

The Interlink between (a) the Events of the Canal Extension Act 1829 & Topsham Lock and (b) the Events precipitating the 1840 Act

leaving the Navigation committee to cover the whole of the rest of the river and estuary, as well also as the Exeter Ship Canal, as it then had become "upgraded" in name.

The Map showing the limits of the TRCs jurisdiction under the 1840 Act is included in the Maps Section at the beginning of this Book, preceding Chapter One.

It might well be presumed that post-1829, the Chamber and its successor Exeter City Council ("ECC") from 1835 were more focussed on the Canal extension and the development of its shipping trade direct up to Exeter quay/basin, rather than continuing with the parallel use of the navigable channel between Topsham Lock and Turf Pool, if only because of the doubling of maintenance expenses which they had engendered.

So, when faced with such double expenses and perhaps being "battered" by the continuing complaints from the Topsham Quay's merchants and traders, as to the Chamber's neglect of its dredging and Quay maintenance obligations, which were heard and sympathetically recorded and upheld by the Commissioners in their 1834 Report into the Exeter Chamber's affairs (see Chapter Ten and Appendix 8), it might have served the Chamber / ECC well to "offload" the Topsham channel and all dredging and Quay maintenance liabilities upon a new body, such as came so shortly afterwards to be created by the 1840 Act, when the Port of Topsham River Commissioners became charged with such dredging, per Clause 75 of the 1840 Act. The City was engaged in "outsourcing" its responsibilities – and liabilities.

The other aspect of having the two sets of maintenance obligations on the part of the Chamber /ECC was that the Canal extension was not a natural "Cut" but one created by building raised artificial embankments which had caused great unforeseen expenses in its construction and which required considerable maintenance, (including having to increase the heights of the Banks to ensure the increased depth of water required at 12 feet), with risks of severe weather conditions and flooding, as exemplified in the great storm of unprecedented vigour and destruction of Monday 22nd November 1824 during its very construction, causing havoc to the Works and all the surrounding low lying marshes and water meadows. The problems encountered in constructing Turf Lock are a story unto themselves.

As previously detailed, the Topsham River Commissioners comprised the four elected local Inhabitants and the three appointed direct by the Exeter City Council from amongst their Council Members. Their function was designed as a balancing body between Town and City and might best be described as a form of local devolution, in order to give a strong local voice and responsibility to Topsham, whilst under the strategic authority of the City as the port authority (as defined in the 1840 Act). In more modern phrasing, it might have been thought better to have the Topsham traders brought within the City

Tent, rather than complaining and causing mischief outside its Canvas.

Whilst not the subject of this Book, it is to be noted that the Tolls problems and resulting disputes caused by the Chamber in increasing the Fees for the Ship Canal because of the Extension and then trying to inflict the increases upon the Shipowners and inhabitants of Exeter in order to pay off the huge debts they had engendered was the subject of acrimony and challenge by the Citizens of the City. Whilst it was stated by the Chamber, especially by Mr R R Sanders, that the Income from the Extension and accruing to the Chamber might have increased, the persuasive challenge made was that this was more the result of an increase in the Fees than the increased usage of the Canal - two wholly separate sources of income stream (see Chapters Nine and Ten).

The Tolls situation, apart from the burdens of the general increases upon all users following the Extension to Turf, was resolved by the Clauses in the Canal Extension Act 1829 which established an equality of tolls as between Turf Lock and Topsham Lock, whichever Lock was being used and by any Vessel. (Chapter Five and Appendix 4)

In terms of the Quay Dues, between the two Quays, the problems and areas of dispute were resolved under the 1840 Act by the Equalisation of Quay Dues Clauses incorporated within the Act. (Chapter 1)

CHAPTER THIRTEEN

As at 2023 - the Current Statutory Basis empowering the Port of Exeter

1. **The River Exe Act 1539** *(an "Acte Publicke")*[3]

    The Royal Commission 1688 - (a non-statutory Royal Decree)

2. **The Exeter Port Dues Act 1840** *(a "public Act"- s.40)*

3. **Local Legislation:-**
    (i) **Section 27 Exeter City Council Act 1987** (power to make byelaws to control navigation on the Exe)
    (ii) **River Exe and Exe Estuary Byelaws 1976** (prohibition of speeds in excess of 10 knots, water skiing outside prescribed areas & promotion of safe navigation generally)
    n.b The **Harbours, Docks and Piers Clauses Act 1847** does not apply to the Port of Exeter other than within the Exmouth Docks (which were incorporated as a statutory body under the Exmouth Docks Act 1864).

Because of the statutory power to improve navigation it is stated that Exeter City Council ("ECC") is a statutory harbour authority (not just a franchise harbour) by virtue of its powers under Section 31 of the 1840 Act (see Chapter 1 – Our Provenance). As a result, ECC is empowered to promote a Harbour Revision Order under the **Harbours Act 1964** (as amended) to vary the scope of its powers as Harbour Authority. At the present time, ECC has weak powers over both the River Exe and the Ship Canal, with no powers for the Harbourmaster to make requisite General and Special directions such as to direct vessels.

The Harbourmaster may within his brief from ECC charge Harbour Dues but has no powers to enforce their payment by non-commercial craft, except as a civil debt through the Courts.

The object is to bring the Port into full and updated compliance with the needs and intended purposes within the developing strategy of ECC, through its Harbour Board, for its future within the 21st Century.

[3] *Acta Publica – a public act.*

CHAPTER FOURTEEN
The Last Major Achievement of the TRCs by 2023

In 2022, the TRCs were enabled to fund, using the bulk of their capital monies, the long-awaited buoyage for the up-river from The Goat Walk to Retreat. This was because of the initiative to do so being pursued with patience and vigour by the Harbourmaster, Mr Grahame Forshaw and his Team, working closely with Trinity House and ECC.

The navigational aids are fitted with low intensity lights. Already their use is being appreciated by passing Yachtmen and all others enjoying the River. The naming of the buoys was designed to provide local colour and to pay respects to many who have given service to the River.

MUSEUM (Red: 26) – To honour Topsham Museum in preserving the history of Topsham and the River Exe & Ship Canal. This was laid to replace the previous yellow "No Wash" buoy.

KATIE McCABE (Red: 28) – To honour Katie as the youngest person to have sailed round England, in 2022, (*with multifarious National Award nominations in recognition of her voyage*)

TREVOR G (Green: 47) - To honour Trevor Greenslade, a much respected and late doyen of TSC, a National Champion in the Hornet Class, and a former Yard Marshal & Guardian of the TSC's metaphysical Green Shed.

VOYSEY (Red: 30) To honour a revered and long established Topsham family of fishermen & boatbuilders, with Bannen Voysey a key Town figure as also Eric Voysey, one of his many grandsons, an "Everyman" of Topsham.

NORTON (Red: 32) To honour another long established Topsham family name, including TSC's Jim Norton, a respected "Ancient of Days" and former Commodore, with 42 years of unbroken service as a TRC.

THE CLOCK (Red: 34) This is its known station in the River since time immemorial, named after an established Salmon-fishing "haul" on the River.

THE COMMISSIONERS (Red: 36) To commemorate the TRCs for their services from 1840 to 2023 and continuing into extra time, whereupon they will pass into history upon the enactment of a Harbour Revision Order under the regime of the statutory Port of Exeter's Harbour Board

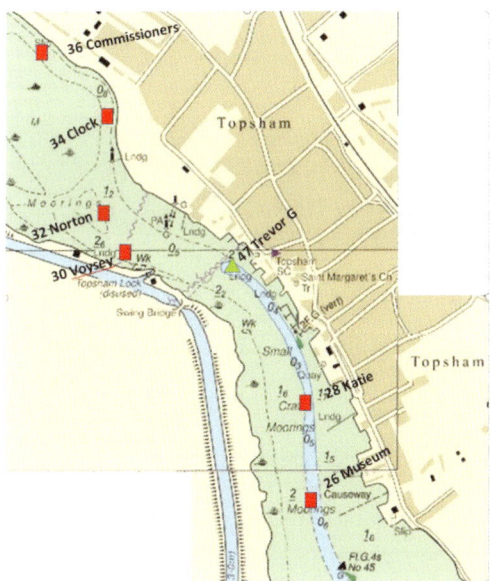

CHAPTER FIFTEEN

[A] A Final Coda and Reflection

There was an ensuing political, economic and historical context to an important part of the 1840 Act, arising from the Extension to develop the Ship Canal (1824/1828), in that the "enforced" construction by the Chamber of the Topsham Lock, after Robert Davy's litigation, was accompanied by the accompanying need and obligation to then secure for commercial navigation a fully cleansed and dredged channel between the Topsham Lock downriver to the Turf Pool where the Canal Extension had been terminated with its new Turf Lock.

Despite all the tensions and drama that had existed between the two Quays at Exeter and Topsham, there is the case that the 1840 Act was a stabilising and "healing" force which brought a more positive and mutually beneficial balance to their future relationships. The construction of Topsham Lock had become the last piece of the historical jigsaw designed to bring the future of the Port of Exeter with its Ship Canal into the Sunny Uplands of commercial prosperity and fortune, whilst the 1840 Act was to prove the pinnacle of the Port's history, but sadly not its fortune, because it was followed by a decline when its commerce and prominence passed over to other Ports and Regions of the Country better suited to the demands of a more industrialised Society, such as in the Midlands and the North.

All personalities and local politics apart, the economic reality was that the dynamics of Waterborne transport had changed. For Exeter, those "exigencies of unforeseen circumstances" arose with disturbing consequences for the City generally and the two Quays in particular, undermining the future of the Port, when, on the 1st May 1844, the Railway Age reached Exeter St David's Station, with the first train arriving from Bristol, hauled by the steam locomotive *The City of Exeter*.

Other commercial and trading developments caused further pressures with competition from Starcross as a potential Railway Port (where the last remaining "stubs" of the wooden railway siding can still be seen on low tide at Cockwood) and also the envisaged Great Western Canal through Topsham to Taunton. Later came the several Extension and Branch Lines including that to

Exmouth Docks, bringing a new and competitive life to that Port. On 1st May 1861 there then came the London & South Western Railway Branch line to Topsham Quay itself.

The Argument that I have pursued in this Book has forced me to conclude that the need to appoint River Commissioners under the 1840 Act would not have been necessary in the first place, being established as a Supplemental body to the already existing powers of the Navigation Committee of the Chamber, **if** the extension of the Canal down to Turf had **not** been embarked upon by the Chamber, despite having received a professional opinion as to a much simpler and less expensive alternative, under James Green's First Report in 1820 (Chapter 4 and Appendix 3).

It is within such context where the personalities, social attitudes and oligarchical view of their place in Exeter Society of Messrs. William Crockett and Robert Rogers Sanders have much to answer for, having regard to the consequences of their persuasive influence and actions, in so doing thereby reaping the wrath of the inhabitants of both City and Town when, in the events that flowed therefrom, their ripening corn turned into a bitter harvest.

For all the argued reasons and recited circumstances, as outlined, it is to Robert Davy that we must grant Honour and pay Homage, for the continuing survival of the Dignity and trading existence of Topsham, he being the man who was the initiator of the Court Case and the financier of the group of five Topsham traders ("the Topsham Five" in modern Protest parlance) who brought the legal case against the Exeter Chamber (Chapter Seven and Appendix 5), without which there would have been no Agreement dated 26th March 1829, (Chapter Eight) whereunder Topsham Lock came to be constructed, followed as a consequence by the Exeter Port Dues Act 1840, which brought the Port of Topsham River Commissioners into being, of which statutory body it is my privilege to serve as Clerk and which, in its own turn, is the basis for the Fragments within this Book, as a simple attempt to "pierce the bubble" of our creation and existence, before we fade away on the ebb leaving but a few shards of Memory, to find our resting place on Estuary Mud.

[B] The Demise of the Port of Topsham River Commissioners

It being so recognised that our existence will cease as soon as a new HRO is enacted, the TRCs will be obliged to provide a full Account to the Harbour Board and the City of Exeter for the balance of funds then in hand, as well as handing over the Minute books and Records as then being held, noting that the earliest Records are already in the safe custody of the Devon Heritage Centre.

At that point of Enactment of the HRO, it might possibly have no more reason to be said of the Topsham River Commissioners and their History than that:

When the Winds of History passeth over the Estuary,
We shall Vanish
And the Place thereof shall know us no more....

T R Epton, M.A. (Cantab)

The Clerk to the Topsham River Commissioners for the Port of Exeter

Afterword

Standfast today in its benign solemnity, Topsham Lock presents two faces to our current generations, each valid unto itself if not also speaking alternative truths. I am conflicted, with my near 70 years in the Law carrying all the marks or stigmata of seeing both sides of the Argument, whilst recognising that certain cases or situations are incapable of mediation or the wisdom of a "judicious compromise". Here, there is no fence upon which to sit, as arguably, say, there might be with the Elgin Marbles, where a Case could be argued and settled, on amicable terms, that the Marbles should be returned to their homeland in Greece but with eye-deceiving Replicas quietly substituted in their place at The British Museum. This is just an example – I am making no personal case either way.

Here in Topsham, the situation can be viewed in simple, if brutal, terms. **Either** Topsham Lock should be fully restored into its former working and operational order **or** it should be left to the Passage of Time in its present state of passive decay and conscious neglect. Maintaining it as a "Folly" in a condition of a "picturesque decline" simply leaves a structure that is of no Use or Purpose unless perceived as an Ornament to the Eye.

I will attempt to articulate both sides of the case, leaving each Reader to consider their own point of view. *Quot homines, tot sententiae…*[4]

To make the case for just "letting things be", ("*the Doctrine of Romantic Decay*"), I bring to mind when, some decades ago, I had occasion to be in the Hill Station of Dalhousie, Himachal Pradesh, India, with Tibetan friend Rikkha-la, where amongst the 'Highlands of Scotland landscape' with its fine Scottish-Baronial Summer Houses from the Raj Era of the British Empire, we came across one such fine residence, enshrined in foliage and brambles, unoccupied and derelict. I was told that it had belonged to Moti Lal Nehru, the father of Jawaharlal Nehru, as the family's Summer Residence, whose fastidious ways had to be observed to the letter. When I expressed amazement that it was left abandoned without any Blue Plaque of fame nor had entered into the arms of an Indian National Trust, Rikkha-la smiled and said "In England you preserve Everything – here in India, All Things shall Pass".

---

[4] *There are as many opinions as there are people: each has his own correct way*

Everything has its moment and then it shall be allowed its natural decay.

Also, for some years, I had further occasion to be living in the City of Bath, Somerset, at a time when many (but not all) of the Georgian artisan quarters were being demolished and there came a cultural energy for the fine Georgian Houses to be cleaned, conserved, renovated and modernised to reach the conundrum of their 20th Century residents wanting to live within the elegance and grandeur of a Georgian/ Regency England but with all modern conveniences to boot. I intend no point but simply make the observation, with the query -Does this make Life "Authentic" or "Artificial"? If many Blue Plaques represent the "Past", then where is the "Now" in between their Facades? Is there a middle way to navigate? To what extent do current generations want to live in a "Museum Town or City" - a Cardboard City of facades, as if created for a Film Set?

It was only recently, when age has allowed more reflective and shrinking time to consider such matters, that my thoughts felt obliged to move from the "Vale of Contemplation" towards the "Valley of Decision", as to which side of my self-constructed Fence I wanted to rest, in how we view our Past from the 21st Century. There is so much information and records of Local History now available, as with the City of Exeter and the Town of Topsham, say, to provide a perspective from which to consider these questions, even if in fragments for each of us to assemble as we might choose.

In part, I have been taking into account that a budget for a proper reconstruction and re-gating of Topsham Lock could now cost in excess of £2m, granted also that under the Canal Extension Act there is an obligation upon ECC to maintain the Lock in full working order in perpetuity. (See Chapter Five).

If indeed Topsham Lock were to be so restored, then I would ask, who would actually use it again, granted that there is no longer the former commercial traffic for which it had been constructed and designed to serve? ('*the Doctrine of Practical Reality*')

Would it be operated by enthusiastic volunteers, clothed in 19th century working garments?

Would Topsham Lock Cottage serve Victorian teas made to original recipes? A working museum piece, full of historic "character" and imagination?

This fantasy in turn needs to take into account that one of the principal aims of the Harbour Board is to promote, for accepted and publicly declared good reasons, the development of a fuller recreational and leisure usage of both the River and the Canal, leading to the ensuing point that it might well then become arguable that, in the 21st century, such Estuary and Port usage has indeed the function to establish its own, newer commercial base, so that the Harbour Board can cover all its own expenditures, overheads and programmes, as well also all new liabilities to be undertaken, in order for its role not to become a loss-making burden that would be placed upon the local population and ratepayers at large.

Even if this Vision were not required to be profit-making *per se*, its Accounts could be "ring-fenced" so as not to support any other non-Estuary, River and Canal budget Accounts of ECC. If this is a reasonable position, then who might object to such a self-sustaining and self-financing strategy?

To focus this view upon Topsham Lock and listening to the voices of those senior inhabitants of Topsham who have navigated it when in its working days, it is considered that Topsham Lock, granted its modest size, was a very "agreeable" and straightforward Lock to use, in technical terms, in contrast to the larger Lock at Turf, with its heavier Gates. Topsham Lock carries a "friendly feel" to it, with its delightful Lock Cottage, as still sought out so often by artist and photographer. Topsham Lock is "picturesque" apart from its intended function – in this fulfilled case, one then of both Use and Ornament!

To fulfil a greater usage, a restored Lock would need to be served by a Topsham Channel that would need to be dredged once more, noting that, again, this was provided for as an obligation upon ECC under the 1840 Act (See Chapters One and Eleven), albeit discharged through the remit of the Topsham River Commissioners.

Whatever the present state of affairs, perhaps we could learn from the keynote mantra of Giuseppe Tomasi di Lampedusa's masterpiece, "Il Gattopardo" (The Leopard): "Things must change, in order that they can remain the same."

Might this mantra offer a Middle Path through the problem of either allowing decay or seeking a reconstruction, one that would avoid the pastiche of a heritage-themed "Project", if the object was to restore a **working Lock for 21st Century use** rather than a "Living Museum" edifice?

Now, in 2023, standing apart from all previously held views and opinions, which might well be overtaken by future events (both known and unknown), let us take into account the forebodings induced by Climate Change, for which Dawlish Warren and the Estuary are on notice as being vulnerable and prone to allowing a major catastrophe of flooding and destruction reaching right up to Exeter itself.

If such fears become hardened and justified, then a case might well emerge that posits the closing down of Turf Lock and the artificially embanked Extension section of Canal up to Topsham Lock, which then, when reconstructed, would become the Haven Pool for the southerly end of the Canal. The very construction of that Extension Section and the Turf Lock itself, under the James Green Second Report 1824, had been faced with major problems in their technical execution, apart from having increased the budget costings which had placed the Chamber in such critical financial difficulty. The Great Flood of the Winter of 1824 caused havoc beyond prediction, as the Canal Extension Works were "lost" in the flooding of both River and also the adjoining marshes and water meadows which are at much lower level – explaining why the Section's embankments are required to be so high.

It would indeed become ironic if, in the fullness of the next decades, such a change did come to pass, whereby, with Topsham Lock then fully restored, Topsham can offer its Salutations to the memory of its local Hero, Robert Davy, without whom the Topsham Lock would never have been constructed, the 1840 Act with its Topsham River Commissioners never enacted and this Book would never have been required to be written. Such is the turn of the Wheel!

To answer my own Questioning?
I would hope to envisage Topsham Lock being restored into full operational use in the fullness of Time -
- but not necessarily in my Lifetime…

Tom Epton

"Carve the Runes, then be Content with Silence"

Appendix 1

The Historical Context (National)

These times (1800 to 1850) saw a plethora of fundamental changes that need to be considered when narrowed down to provide the context of the Exe Estuary and the daily life of its population. Worthy of note is that the Population of Exeter in 1700 was around some 11,500 and in 1800 it had "only" increased to some 17,000 (and the bulk of that possibly achieved by 1750), with a changing of its class structure as the middle classes, in their own degrees, started to more strongly emerge at the expense of the old working class which had been principally engaged in the woollen trade in all its aspects, particularly in its fulling and dyeing activities. At the time of the 1834 Commissioners' Report it was stated to be 28,242 (1831).

Society as a whole was adjusting to breaking away from its feudalistic and agrarian structure as a rural society towards that of an urban society propelled by the Industrial Revolution and the growth of cities, re-enforced by the effects of the Enclosure Movements upon the agricultural population. In rural Devon, rather than in the industrial North and Midlands, Exeter became somewhat caught in the middle of this national adjustment, having lost its trading prominence without any equivalent mercantile substitution. The Port had served its former trading times and purposes.

In the case of the Monarchy, the period from 1800 to 1850 encompasses four sovereigns, from George III, George IV, William IV to Victoria – which represents a state of monarchical "flux" as opposed to the following 64 years of monarchical stability with Victoria and then our own recent 70 years with Elizabeth II from 1952 to 2022.

Political unrest, including the Chartists movement and the Corn Laws upheavals, led to the Great Reform Act 1832, with its opening-up of the electoral franchise and the wholesale removal of the Rotten Boroughs and the oligarchical powers for local administrations, accompanied by the subsequent murmurings of educational provision for the working people. (Note the creation of the London Mechanics Institute in 1823, as an early example).

This fundamental change at the National parliamentary level was followed by the wholesale re-organisation of local Government, as embedded in the Municipal Corporations Act 1835, which in the case of the Exeter Chamber meant its being replaced after centuries of oligarchical rule. This must have been of huge political and social significance to the governance of Estuary life, including more public accountability and a greater democratic tone for the local society.

How so much of events in this period can be interpreted by our own generation at this local level must be because of the local Press and the detailed way in which so much evidence is contained in their reportage, especially of local governmental affairs and Law Reports. The local press, such as *The Western Times, the Exeter Flying Post, the Exeter and Plymouth Gazette* are classic examples of expanding a community's lines of communication as well as catering for an increasing literacy of the working classes who at that time were forming the vast bulk of the city's population. The local newspaper plus local "gossip" were the sole means of broadcasting secular information, with no electric power, telephone, telex, email, television and "mass media" which colours the modern means of exchange of news and human intercourse, if sadly at the expense of a local press which has become essentially an advertising Sales broadsheet. The 19th Century Press, whatever their political stances were indeed "the Voice of the People" for mass communication at that time, in the way that, in the 21st Century, Facebook and Twitter et al. are not, reducing everything to predictive shorthand words and abbreviated conversation ... perhaps Words in conversation are beginning to lose their purpose?

Religious toleration entered the picture, for both Roman Catholics and Dissenters, with the abolition of the Test Acts as one part. Universities admitted non-Anglicans, whilst Methodism gained deep roots – with particular reference and interest to local Methodists amongst the important traders and merchants of Topsham.

In a national context, the Victorian Age witnessed a plethora of statutory legislation to cope with increasingly sophisticated needs and expectations, within a fast-growing industry-based population that was starting to benefit from such increased literacy and religious tolerances across all classes of society. As with the shift from a rural to an industrial society, so also developed a transfer towards a more centralised form of government, administering by national Statute Laws of Parliament at the expense of the Common Law based on precedents to be followed as a fundamental principle, although a Case was capable of being decided on the facts of each particular case – which is where Equity enters the picture in English Law and the Court of Chancery receives cautionary mention in Chapter Seven, in respect of Robert Davy's Court Case.

The structure of the legal system also became subject to a fundamental series of changes with a more secular emphasis developing, at the expense, say, under the Civil Law of the jurisdiction of the Ecclesiastical Courts, with the areas of wills and probates gradually becoming more of a State rather than a religious function for the Ecclesiastical Courts. In general, there was the beginning of a more formal development of Public Administrative Law, one that is continuing to this present day and age.

Finally, in terms of our Empire, as its dynamic began its mercantile movement away from the Caribbean towards the Far East and India in particular, the Abolition of the Slave Trade in 1807 was followed by the Act for the Abolition of Slavery itself in 1833, perhaps in part for economic reasons rather than solely humanitarian. The shift from the mercantilism of the 17th and 18th centuries towards free trade in the 19th century is a subject in its own right when studying the trade along the Estuary. One event of importance and benefit to the Exeter traders had been an Act of 1698 under William 3rd relating to free trade and "Encouraging the Woollen Manufacturers of this Kingdom" but whilst still preserving the Monopolies of those Companies with their Charters for the Levant, Eastland (largely Baltic-Scandinavia), Russia and Africa *(n.b. the Monopoly of the Royal Africa Company, founded in 1672, and its role in the Slave Trade, with certain Royal connections and endorsements).*

Whilst England was seeing the emerging benefits of both its Empire and an industrialised 19th Century Capitalism, as the Enclosure Movements were changing the lives of the rural population, the continuing tragedy of our relationship with Ireland, which became part of the United Kingdom in 1801, started to unfold, leading to the Great Famines of 1845-1852, with one million Irish deaths from disease and poverty whilst another million sought refuge in emigration. Such disturbing events are an integral part of the national context framing daily lives with our own localities, with the Navigators of both Canals and Railways, for example, so often being cloaked with generic anonymity, simply as "Irish navvies". We know that William Crockett masterminded the Canal Extension – but who did the actual digging?

Exeter was not immune to all these changes, particularly in the economic sphere where its historic role and wealth from the woollen trade essentially collapsed after 1815, despite the dominant role it had held in the 17th and earlier three-quarters of the 18th Centuries. That was Exeter's "Golden Age" of prosperity. All these aspects are worthy of note for the effect that they came to have upon the port of Exeter and its commercial prosperity (once the hub of the city's wealth and prestige) and its future viability. How did individual citizens absorb, witness or adjust to these events as they cascaded down through the first half of the 19th Century? What was the level of these changes, coming in such complex volume as an "assault" upon their daily lives and their respective levels of literacy, prosperity and social status? We can only catch fragments of so many unheard voices and written evidence from ordinary people, who experienced their own working lives without the power with which the more educated and entitled in society were privileged to enjoy.

Appendix 2

Exeter & Plymouth Gazette – Extracts from the Revd. George Oliver's essay on Early Navigation of the Exe &c. (1826).

By an Inquisition taken at Exeter, 29th August, 1290, before Malcolm de Harleigh, General Escheator of King Edward I, it was satisfactorily shewn that the course of the river Exe from as far up the stream as Exeter Bridge, was originally the property of the Crown; that the city of Exeter was also an appurtenance to the Crown; that King Henry III had granted the same to his brother, Richard, Earl of Cornwall; that the citizens held the fee-farm of the said city of Richard aforesaid, as they had holden it formerly of the Crown, by the yearly payment of £13.9s.: that in virtue of such grant, and of ancient custom, the Exe water belongs to the said city, as far down as the port of Exmouth; that the right of fishing and of using the waterway was common to all; that Isabella, Countess of Devon, in the year 1284, erected a lofty wear across the bed of the river at Topsham, which prevented the taking of salmon and other fish above the said wear, to the great damage of the city and neighbourhood; and that whereas boats *(batelli)* were accustomed to come up to Exeter bridge, with wines and merchandize, to the singular advantage of the city and surrounding country, no boats at present reach the city by reason of the said wear. A verdict was recorded in favor of the city.

Notwithstanding this triumph of reason and justice, the navigation of the river was further impeded, and the trade of the city greatly diminished by Isabella's heir, Hugh, Lord Courtenay, the first of that powerful family who was Earl of Devonshire. He built a quay at Topsham, the general receiving place of the city's customs, and his bailiffs obstructed the city's serjeants in the execution of their right of searching and stopping vessels, The citizens very frequently preferred complaints against the illegal encroachments; and though they successfully maintained their right to tolls, as part and appurtenance to the fee-farm of their city, on all imports, and though as their Court Rolls demonstrate, they frequently seized and condemned vessels that presumed, without the licence, and against the liberty of the city, to discharge their cargoes at Prattyshede[5] (alias Exmouth), at Le Torffe or Turf, at Lympstone, at Powderham, and at Colepole; yet partly owing to the confusion of the times, and partly to the overwhelming influence of the Courtenay interest, the removal of the wear could not be accomplished. Nay, Holingshed asserts that Edward Courtenay, Earl of Devon, who died in 1419 succeeded in spite of all opposition to erect two other wears, viz. St. James's Wear, extending across the river, (but which continued to be a stake wear only until the year 1811) and another at Lampreford. All such wears had been expressly forbidden by Magna Charta as public nuisances; but though they produced the main obstruction to the free navigation of the Exe we must also bear in mind, that the citizens, in their petition to King Henry VIII in the course of the year 1539, enumerate other causes, viz. "dryvings of sands and gravell by course of the water, the high spring tides, and the floods of freshwater coming into the said river." Perhaps stream-works or tin-works may have also contributed to increase the evil. To provide a remedy, partial but ineffectual attempts were made from the year 1540, to open a watercourse called "The Haven or New Work," to which Leland alludes, (fol. 64, vol.1, itinerary) thus "Men of Excestre contend to make the Haven to cum up to Excestre self. At this tyme shippes cum not farther up but to Apsham" *(Now called Topsham).*

In the reign of Edward VI, the labor was continued, and several parishes in the city contributed their church plate towards the expences of the undertaking; but learn from p.276 of Fuller's Worthies that in the summer of 1594 considerable damage was done to the river in the direction of Mount Wear, by the rebels who besieged Exeter. The great increase of commerce with the Low Countries, Italy, and Spain, during the reign of Queen Mary, and her incorporation of the merchants of Exeter, on the 4th May, 1556, excited the spirit of enterprise and made the want of water communication with Topsham, to be more severely felt; but the shortness and the troubles of her government prevented anything effectual from being accomplished. At length, in 1560, Wm. Strode, Esq. tendered proposals to the Mayor and corporation for making a canal to convey boats of eight tons burthen to the city. Three years later, viz. 21st Sept. 1563, the plans of John Trewe, an engineer of Glamorganshire, were finally approved and adopted, and under his direction, and by the aid of seven sluices, lighters of sixteen tons burthen were enabled to ascend this navigable canal and discharge their cargoes at the Water-Gate: the expence of the undertaking amounted to £5000. This engineer is still remembered by the

---

[5] *The Ferry at Pratteside or Pratteshede, or Exmouth, has belonged, to the Mayor and Chamber from time immemorial. In October, 1287 they leased to John Pycard, possagium nostrum de Pratteshide, to hold the same at their pleasure under the yearly rent of 4s. with the obligation of his keeping in good repair domus nostras, battelum illius passagii.*

wear that bears his name (though in early deeds it is often called St. Leonard's wear); and his "New work or Haven," as it is styled in a document of 16th. Feb. 1592, ranks him amongst the very first, as well as the ablest projectors of inland navigation, in the United Kingdom. How ill-informed must the writer be in the Bengal Hurkaru, of 4th Dec 1823, p.231, who considers that the canal to bring coals from St. Helen's to Liverpool, for which the commercial and enterprising inhabitants of the latter place obtained an Act of Parliament in 1755, "was the first canal with locks that ever was constructed in Great Britain."

After the restoration of King Charles II, it was found that the works of Quay, Wharf and Haven, had been shamefully neglected by the lessees, George, Gilbert and John Clare, to whom the Mayor and Council had leased them on 20th Dec. 1654 for a term of 21 years. The King had issued his Commission to constitute Exeter a royal port: this circumstance gave new energy to commercial interests, and application was made to Parliament to widen and improve the canal. The work was begun soon after the expiration of the Clares' lease, at Christmas, 1675, with extraordinary zeal and spirit, and was seconded by the public with laudable emulation. Amongst the most influential and active promoters of this useful undertaking, was Dr. George Cary, Dean of Exeter. A damp, however, was thrown on the enterprise by the fraudulent conduct of the engineer, Wm. Bailey, of Winchester, who decamped with a considerable sum of money. Mr. Daniel Dennell, afterwards I believe one of the projectors of the water-works, and Mr Gilbert Greenslade were subsequently engaged to superintend and forward the arduous undertaking.

It was occasionally interrupted, however, for want of ways and means; and the Act Books plainly shew, that the Chamber submitted to many painful sacrifices in order to prosecute and accomplish this laborious and expensive work. According to Prince (p.215, New Edn. of Worthies) nearly £20,000 had been expended on the business up to the year 1699. Though the canal was actually passable, still new improvement were suggested and adopted, until, at last in the early part of the year 1725 "THE PORT WAS OPENED."

The new Archbishop of York, Dr. Lancelot Blackburne (who before his translation had been Bishop of Exeter for nearly eight years), Lord Chief Justice King, Lord Walpole, and many other distinguished personages, were invited to join at this joyful ceremony. The canal was then computed to be about three miles and a quarter in length, and brought trade and wealth for many years to the merchants of Exeter.

Andrew Brice, in his Topographic Dictionary[6] assures us that in the year 1750, the amount of woollen goods, corn, and hides, shipped from this port, rose to the astonishing sum of one million sterling. And the Act of George II, ch.8, for opening the port of Exeter for the importation of wool and woollen

---

[6] Brice, Andrew, *The Grand Gazetteer or Topographic Dictionary*, Printed by and for the author, Exeter, 1759.

yarn from Ireland, must have contributed to increase this prosperity, until the subsequent wars with America and France inflicted a deep wound on all commercial enterprise.

Appendix 3[7]

Extracts from the Minutes of the Proceedings of The Institution of Civil Engineers, Transactions Vol. IV, session 1845, with Abstracts of the Discussions and with John Green's Reports as a Continuation of the Memoir of the Canal of Exeter, from 1563 to 1724, by Philip Chilwell De la Garde, including the relevant Appendices (A) and (B) therewith.

18th February 1845 Sir JOHN RENNIE, President, in the Chair.

No.671. "Memoir of the Canal of Exeter, from 1563 to 1724" by Philip Chilwell De la Garde with a Continuation by James Green, M.Inst.C.E.

> ... *(here follows the ending of Philip C de la G's Memoir, of 1834, ending with the following "Eulogy/Econium/Epitaph/Apologia" in praise of the Exeter Chamber and its virtues, of which he himself (an Ophthalmic Surgeon) had been a Member and also its last Mayor, in 1835).*
>
> "... Sympathy is due for the Chamber of that day, whose opinions were far too in advance, not only of their city, but of the Legislature. It was no small matter for a corporate body, in a corner of the empire, to conceive and attempt (more than 50 years before the Sankey Cut), a canal of 10 feet in depth – a canal, in all other respects, coinciding with the still greater work, which they were enabled to complete before their final extinction in 1835, and which remains a monument of the courage, integrity, and zeal, with which, for 700 years, they had directed the commercial affairs of their city."
>
> *(This degree of self-praise and self-justification invites the Reader to Compare and Contrast an alternative view of things, as explored in Chapter Nine, "Hubris & Nemesis")*

No. 671A. "Continuation of the Memoir of the Canal of Exeter, from 1819 to 1830." By James Green, M. Inst. C. E.

"As Mr. De la Garde's Memoir, which embraces so clear an historical account

---

[7] *Note that all comments in this section, whether in italics, highlights or under-linings are the author's.*

of the first formation of the Exeter Canal, and its successive improvements and extensions, closes with a reference to its imperfect condition in the year 1819, and mentions the Reports subsequently made thereon, it may not be unacceptable to the Institution to be succinctly informed of the state of the canal at that period, and what has been done, since that time, to render it a ship canal, capable of passing vessels of 500 tons burden quite up to the city of Exeter. Previous to the year 1820, the canal had been for many years, only capable of passing vessels drawing 9 feet of water from the tideway of the river Exe, about a mile above the town of Topsham, to the quays in the river Exe, at Exeter; but the increase in the size of the canal, although accomplished by great perseverance, on the part of the Chamber, and at a vast expense, had been effected in a very imperfect manner, and the several works had become greatly impaired and dilapidated.

The canal from the King's Arms sluice, at its entrance into the Exe, near the city, to what is called the 'double lock,' and which is nearly on the site of the highest, or third sluice, or pool, described in the memoir, was a level pond. It had been originally so constructed, that the water should be 10 feet deep, but the banks had been much washed down, (Section No. 2, Plate 2).

The double lock had become greatly decayed, although it was still capable of passing several vessels simultaneously.

The course of the canal, from the tail of this double lock, to its entrance into the tideway, above Topsham, which was about 2 miles in length, was nearly the same as at present; at its junction with the tideway there was a sluice, *(n.b. this is the Lower Sluice) w*ith only one pair of gates, pointing inwards, so that vessels could only pass this sluice, when the water in the pond above it, was level with the tide outside the gates, and as the bed of this lower pond of the canal formed the only outlet for the several brooks which constituted the exclusive drainage of an extensive tract of meadow land, it was requisite that this accumulation of water should flow away every low tide.

The cill of this sluice was laid 2 feet above the bed of the tidal channel; and the level of the lower gate cill of the double lock was 4 feet higher than the cill of the lower sluice; so that it was necessary to raise this lower pond of the canal for 2 miles in length, with water, at least 4 feet deep, drawn from the upper pond of the canal, before a vessel, which was carried by the tide over the cill of the lower sluice, could pass that of the double lock. This lower pond of the canal might therefore be aptly compared to a lock 2 miles in length, with a rise of at least 4 feet. The disadvantages of such a mode of ship navigation, to an important commercial city, may be easily conceived. The first, and perhaps the most important object, was to repair the double lock, and in doing this, care was taken so to lower the cills of the gates, as to facilitate any further improvements in the canal which might be considered desirable.

In October, 1820, *[James Green's First Report]* in a very full report on the state of the canal, and the improvements of which it was capable, it was shown that the increasing trade of the city required that vessels, drawing at least 10 feet of water, should approach the quays with facility. This report recommended, that the lower reach of the canal, from the double lock to the tideway of the river, should be converted into a regular pond; that side channels and culverts under the canal should be constructed, so that the brooks, which drained the marshes into the tideway, should be enabled to traverse beneath the canal, by means of these side channels and culverts. **The erection of an entire new lock, with complete gates,** a little lower down the tideway **than the then lower and very imperfect sluice, was also recommended.**

The subsequent improvements were chiefly confined to repairing the banks and bridges, and dredging the upper pond of the canal, until 1824 *[James Green's Second Report]* when the demands for a more perfect navigation become so general, that the authorities were constrained to enter on an entire revision of the works, and as it was evident, for the interest of the trade of the city, that facilities should be given for bringing up larger vessels, further surveys were made, and on the 1st of March, 1824, a report was presented, stating that it would be practicable to extend the canal to Turf, two miles lower down the estuary, **than had before been contemplated** *(i.e. James Green's First Report 1820),* and to which point vessels drawing 12 feet water could navigate on all tides. This report was approved and adopted, and the works were soon afterwards commenced.

In executing these works, it was necessary to carry a considerable portion of the extended line over mud-lands, which were overflowed by the sea at every tide; much difficulty was therefore experienced in maintaining the embankments to the required height, and some extraordinary high tides and floods which occurred, having made extensive breaches in the shore, which separates the estuary from the sea, near Exmouth [*i.e. the Dawlish Warren and Pole Sand]* it was found that the tide rose several feet higher within the estuary, than it had been accustomed to do, before these breaches in the sands had occurred. In consequence of this, it became necessary to raise the embankments over the mud lands 3 feet higher than had been originally intended. *(See Afterword, as to possible future problems arising from Climate Change).*

The raising of these banks, on such a foundation, was a work of considerable difficulty and expense, and it could only proceed slowly; but its completion being imperative, it was accomplished by the persevering energies of the Chamber. This induced the idea and the determination of increasing the depth of water in the canal to 15 feet *(i.e. an increase over the 12 feet originally planned under the Extension to Turf proposal),* and of constructing the entrance lock at Turf, of dimensions adapted to vessels drawing 14 feet of water; hence also arose the necessity of adapting all other parts of the canal to vessels of that class.

These works would have been in a great measure useless, unless the larger class of vessels could arrive at the river basin at Exeter; an entire new and walled basin, capable of accommodating such vessels, independently of the river, was therefore made at the upper end of the canal, close to the city, and was opened for trade on the 29th of September, 1830. Experience has shown, that this increase of the depth of water in the canal, was not greater than was necessary. It was found during the progress of the works, that as the depth of water in the canal increased from time to time, the demands for a still greater depth became more urgent, and the success of the exertions of what may almost be called a private corporate body "in a corner of the kingdom," is proved, by the fact, that the revenues of the canal have trebled since the commencement of the extension of the works *(to be challenged at the time by reason of the severe increase in the Canal Tolls and Dues and the increase in population being served rather than the Extension Works per se)* – see the relevant Chapter.

The only Act of Parliament obtained by the Chamber was passed in 1829, for legalizing the tolls. This Act provided for a lock between the canal and the river Exe at Topsham, which was accordingly executed, so that the necessity for land carriage between Topsham and Exeter was entirely superseded." *(James Green then proceeds with the saga of problems encountered in the construction of Turf Lock, which is not relevant to this Book).*

The piece ends with … "The principal circumstances attendant on the progressive extension and enlargement of the canal, since the year 1820, are detailed in the several reports which are appended, with two reports made by Mr Telford, relative to the Works.

It is worthy of remark, that so early as the year 1698, the Chamber of Exeter contemplated the extension of their canal to Turf, the point at which it now enters the estuary of the Exe (as stated in the memoir), and that they were only foiled in their attempts to effect this, by a successful opposition to an Act of Parliament for the purpose. It is also somewhat extraordinary, that this fact remained unnoticed until it was discovered by Mr de la Garde, in 1834, while preparing his memoir". *(n.b. This stated opposition to the intentions of the Chamber in 1698 showed the common sense and wisdom of the inhabitants of Exeter at that time in foreseeing the consequences of and avoiding the financial disaster that followed the improvidence and imprudence, under their increased oligarchical powers, of the Chamber in 1824, and the consequences of the Extension to Turf Pool thereby engendered)* - as further explored in Chapters Nine and Ten.

Summary of Reports on the Exeter Ship canal from 1820 to 1826.
[Relevant Extracts from] REPORT (A). October, 1820.

"In Mr. James Green's Report, (A), it is shown that the canal was very much out of repair, and its construction up to that time was very imperfect. The site of the lower sluice had been ill chosen, inasmuch as vessels could only enter the canal at spring tides. The channel (*i.e. the artificial Tide-channel/ Back Gut*) from the sluice into the Tide-channel (*i.e. the main navigable Topsham channel*) was very intricate, and was much obstructed by shoals. Imported goods were frequently obliged to be unloaded at Topsham and conveyed by land to Exeter.

The mode in which the lower sluice had been constructed, with only one pair of gates, was another and most serious impediment to the navigation of the canal. The first reach of the canal, from the lower sluice to the double lock, nearly two miles in length, was altogether useless when the tide was out, as it was absolutely necessary to empty this pond at low water on each tide, for the purpose of draining the meadow lands on its borders. This pond or reach at the top of high water, was only 9 feet in depth at the lower end, and as the cills of the lower gates, at the double lock, were 4 feet higher than those at the lower sluice, it was necessary to draw a quantity of water down from the upper pond of the canal into the lower pond, so as to raise the latter for its whole length, in order that such vessels as could pass the lower sluice might enter the double lock. The expense and delay of passing vessels up to Exeter was, under such circumstances, very great.

The hindrance in passing vessels from Exeter to the tideway was, from the same cause, fully as great, if not more so, than in the ascending trade; for it frequently happened that descending vessels were unable, from the falling away of the tide, to get out of the canal, and they were obliged to ground in it, and to wait the return of the tide, which very often did not rise sufficiently high to take them out; in such cases they remained several days in the lower part of the canal, obstructing the entrance of vessels of a smaller class: or if they succeeded in getting through the sluice whilst there was sufficient tide, they would ground on the shoals of the Tide-channel below (*i.e. the Back Gut*) and would thus also prevent other vessels from getting up even to the entrance of the lower sluice. The cost of keeping, even in moderate repair, a tidal channel of two miles in length, and acting at the same time as a main drain to the country, was enormous, as compared with an uniform pond of canal constantly filled with water.

The double lock, constructed with two sets of gates, but without side walls, answered its intended purpose, by passing several vessels at the same time, and the loss of water occasioned by it, was not materially felt, as there was an ample supply from the river Exe.

The canal, from the double lock to the King's Arms sluice, was a regular pond of canal, originally well-constructed; but its course was somewhat tortuous, the depth of water in many places was not more than 8 feet, and great expense was incurred in dredging, in order to pass a vessel drawing more than 9 feet of water. The King's Arms sluice was designed to prevent the flood-water of the river Exe from passing down the canal, but as it had only one pair of gates, vessels in flood times were detained some days, before they could pass this sluice.

The river Exe above King's Arms sluice, which is ponded to the level of the quay-walls on its banks, by Trew's Weir, was a fine natural river basin; but the vessels experienced great inconvenience and delay, not only by floods, but by the difficulty of keeping an uniform depth of water, which could only be done by dredging at a great expense.

The masonry of the lower sluice was greatly dilapidated, and a new set of gates, which had been recently erected, were of a very imperfect construction. The masonry of the double lock was in nearly as bad a state, and the banks, towing-paths, and other works required a thorough repair.

The canal, from the double lock to the King's Arms sluice was recommended to be straightened, and so-far dredged, that there should be at all times a depth of water of 10 feet.

The platform of the lower gates at the double lock, whilst under repair, was recommended to be laid at a lower level, in order to lessen the pressure of water on the gates of the lower sluice, and as new gates would be required, the machinery for moving the paddles was to be made on an improved principle.

It was recommended that the lower sluice, which was constructed on a very imperfect principle, and was in a dilapidated condition, should be rebuilt, with the addition of another or upper pair of gates, so as to convert it into a regular lock; and that the cills of the lower gates should be lowered, so as to be on a level with a permanent shoal across the river, opposite the town of Topsham, as such a proceeding would enable vessels to enter the canal, whenever they could pass that shoal or bar.

It was proposed that the reach from the canal, from its entrance at the lower sluice, to the double lock, should be made a complete and standing pond of water, with a uniform depth of 10 feet.

It was also proposed that the Alphington brook and the drainage of the marsh lands adjoining, for which the course of this part of the canal formed the only outlet to sea, should be provided for, either by a parallel channel on the west side of the canal banks, quite down to the tideway, immediately below the lower sluice, or that the waters should be carried by pipes laid under the canal, and be discharged into the river Exe at an intermediate point.

The various works were recommended to be thoroughly repaired, and the river basin at Exeter to be so dredged, as to have a uniform depth of water of 10 feet in all parts. As the carrying of these works into effect, with a considerable and constant trade through the canal, would occasion a great interruption to that trade, **it was suggested, as an alternative measure, that the site of the new lower sluice should be** <u>**somewhat further down the Tide-channel**</u> **(***i.e. the Back Gut***) between the lower sluice and the river, and that a new cut should be made through the marshes, from the head of this (***i.e. new***) sluice to the canal, somewhat above the existing lower sluice,** with a basin in the cut capable of containing several vessels. The work could be executed whilst the trade of the canal was going on, and besides this advantage, the entrance into the tidal channel would be so much nearer the river, that several intermediate shoals and sudden bends in that channel would be avoided."

(i.e. at the very spot where Topsham Lock came to be constructed after and as a result of the Robert Davy Court Case. The Tide-channel/ Back Gut would have been rendered obsolete and redundant at a stroke – hence this explains why the Jurisdiction of the TRCs came to be limited to the Topsham navigable Channel from Topsham Lock downriver to Turf Pool. The TRCs have no rights or jurisdiction upriver, including over the Tide-channel/ Back Gut.)

(One curious & outstanding matter is why, from 1701 to 1820, no party ever appears to have given the advice that the Single pair of Gates at the Lower Sluice should be replaced by a Double Lock – particularly as the Double Lock had been pioneered upstream, as the first ever in England, with great success. Another little "mystery" is how this 1698 draft Parliamentary Bill for an Extension to Turf came to be "hidden away" for 136 years, until a set of papers was found by chance in a drawer, in 1834, by Mr John Gidley, Esq, the Town Clerk).

[Relevant Extract from] REPORT (B). – March 1st, 1824.

"Mr. Green's Second Report (B), after adverting to the completion of many of the works recommended in the former Report states, that surveys had been made, with a view to ascertain the practicability of carrying the connection of the canal with the estuary of the Exe, **much lower down than had been before contemplated**, and it was recommended, that the canal should be extended to Turf, a point about two miles lower down the river than the original lower sluice, and to which point vessels drawing 12 feet of water could navigate at all tides." *(The two modes of effecting such Extension works down to Turf Pool with a new Lock there were then briefly set out but are not relevant to this Book. Two possible lines for the new Extension were either to have a straight line between the Lower Sluice and Turf Pool or, as came to be the case, to have the line drawn closer to the verge of the river).*

Appendix 4

Extracts from the Canal Extension Act 1829 relating to Topsham Lock

ANNO DECIMO GEORGII IV. REGIS. [Cap. Xlvii]

An Act for altering, extending, and improving the Exeter Canal [14th May 1829]

WHEREAS the Mayor, Bailiffs, and Commonalty of the City of Exeter are the Owners of a navigable Canal which was formed by their Predecessors many Centuries since, for conveying Goods, Wares, and Merchandize, in Barges, Boats, and other Vessels, from the Tideway or navigable Channel of the River Exe above the Town of Topsham in the County of Devon to a Point immediately above the King's Arms Sluice in the Parish of Saint Thomas the Apostle in the same County, so as to join the River Exe at the public and open Quay at Exeter situate in the Parish of the Holy Trinity in the County of the same City: And whereas the said ancient Canal, having been formed very imperfectly, was till lately subject to the Ebb and Flow of the Tide from the said River Exe at its former Entrance through a Sluice called the Lower Sluice situate above the said Town of Topsham, and thereby the Banks of the said Canal were frequently injured, the Repairs thereof rendered expensive, and the Navigation of a considerable Portion of the said Canal liable to great and daily Obstruction, Uncertainty, and Delay: And whereas the said Mayor, Bailiffs, and Commonalty have lately stopped up the aforesaid late Entrance at the Lower Sluice, and have extended the said Canal lower down into the deeper Part of the Tideway or navigable Channel of the said River Exe, to a Place called Turf, below the said Town of Topsham, **and contemplate the opening of a Lock or Entrance above the Town of Topsham, as herein-after mentioned,** and have altered and improved the ancient Part of the said Canal above the said late Lower Sluice, and the said Works are not yet completed; And whereas by stopping up the said Entrance at the Lower Sluice, and extending the said Canal to the present Entrance at Turf as aforesaid, a more certain, expeditious, and easy Communication has already been opened between the Mouth of the

River Exe and the City of Exeter, **and by the said intended Lock above the Town of Topsham the Communication between that Place and the Quay at Exeter will be fully preserved**, and the Completion of the improvements of this Canal will be of great public Utility: And whereas the said Mayor. Bailiffs, and Commonalty, in the Progress of the aforesaid several Works, have expended very large Sums of Money, and are unable properly to complete the same without borrowing further Sums for that Purpose; May it therefore please Your Majesty that it may be enacted; And be it enacted by the King's most Excellent Majesty, by and with the Advice and Consent of the Lords Spiritual and Temporal, and Commons, in this present Parliament assembled, and by the Authority of the same, That the Mayor, Bailiffs, and Commonalty for the Time being of the said City of Exeter, and their Successors and Assigns, Proprietors of the said Canal, shall be and they are hereby authorized and empowered to complete and maintain the said Canal, from the said Kings Arms Sluice in the Parish of Saint Thomas the Apostle in the County of Devon to the said Place called the Turf, below the Town of Topsham in the said County, lately extended and improved as aforesaid, and for that Purpose to keep closed and stopped up the former Entrance into the ancient Part of the said Canal at and through the Lower Sluice, and to substitute in the Stead thereof the present Entrance, at the Extremity of the said extended Canal at Turf, **and also the Lock or Entrance to be opened above the Town of Topsham, as herein-after mentioned** and otherwise to improve the same Canal as herein-after is mentioned, and to do and perform all other Works, Matters, and Things directed and intended to be done and performed, by virtue of this Act, subject to the Rules, Orders, and Directions hereinafter expressed.

II. And be it further enacted, That it shall be lawful for the said Mayor, Bailiffs, and Commonalty, and they are hereby authorized and required, from and after the passing of this Act, by themselves, their Deputies, Agents, Officers, Workmen, and Servants, to open and keep navigable and passable for Boats, Barges, and other Vessels the said Canal so lately extended as aforesaid, from the Tideway or navigable Channel of the River Exe at or near to the said Place called Turf in the Parish of Exminster in the said County of Devon, and **also from a certain intended Entrance into the said Canal from the said navigable River Exe above the Town of Topsham** as herein-after mentioned, into the ancient Part of the said Canal above the late Lower Sluice, and from thence to a Point immediately above the King's Arms Sluice as aforesaid, so as to preserve the aforesaid Communication with the Exeter public Quay, and also to widen the ancient or upper Part of the said Canal, and to strengthen the Banks of the said ancient and extended Canal by widening the same, or otherwise as Occasion shall require, at the several Places mentioned and described in the respective Maps or Plans of the said Canal deposited with the respective Officers of the Clerk of the Peace of the said County of Devon and County of the City of Exeter.

III. And be it further enacted, That the said Mayor, Bailiffs, and Commonalty shall and they are hereby required, within Three Months next after the passing of this Act, **for the Purpose of performing and preserving the Communication by the said Canal between the said City of Exeter and the Tideway of the said River Exe above the said Town of Topsham, to begin to construct and make, and within Two Years next after the passing of this Act as aforesaid to complete and perfect, a proper Lock, of such Dimensions and Construction, and in such Situation within the Distance of Two hundred and sixty Yards above the Bridge opposite to Topsham Ferry, and which Bridge is now placed across the said Canal, as shall be effectual and convenient for the Passage, in, through and out of the same Lock and Canal, of Ships, Vessels, Lighters, Barges, Boats, Craft, and all Goods water-borne of the same Size and Magnitude as could at any Time heretofore pass through the old Canal from the late Lower Sluice before the said Canal was extended as aforesaid; and that after the said Lock shall be made, the same Lock, Gates, Wing Walls, and other Works thereto belonging, shall at all Times for ever hereafter be maintained and kept in good Repair and Condition by the said Mayor, Bailiffs, and Commonalty,** and that the said Lock, and the Gates thereto belonging, shall be under the Control, Management, and Direction of the said Mayor, Bailiffs, and Commonalty, and of such Agent or Agents as they shall from Time to Time appoint for that Purpose: Provided nevertheless, that after the same shall be so completed as aforesaid, it shall be lawful for all Persons, with such Ships, Vessels, Lighters, Barges, Boats, Craft, and all Goods waterborne as aforesaid, to pass at all Times **from and to the Tideway of the said River Exe above the said Town of Topsham, through the said Lock so to be made as aforesaid, into and from the said Canal, and to navigate and use the said Canal to and from the said Lock in as ample and complete a Manner,** and upon Payment of the same Tolls, and subject to the same Regulations as by this Act provided in respect of Ships, Vessels, Lighters, Barges, Boats, Craft, and all Goods waterborne passing to and from the said Canal by the said new Entrance at or near the said Place called Turf.

IX. And whereas, in consequence of the said Canal being immediately adjoining to the River Exe it will be impracticable to build the Bridge communicating with the Horseferry opposite to the Town of Topsham so as to have an Ascent of only One Foot in Thirteen; be it therefore enacted, That nothing herein-before contained shall extend or be construed to extend to the Bridge over the said Canal at the Approach from the Horseferry over the River Exe opposite to the Town of Topsham.

XLVIII. And be it further enacted, That it shall be lawful for the Mayor, Bailiffs, and Commonalty of the said City of Exeter in Common Council assembled, from Time to Time, as and when they may see fit to reduce, apportion, alter, modify, and regulate, and after such Reduction, Alteration, Modification, or Regulation again to raise and increase, and so from Time to Time to reduce, alter, modify, regulate and raise, the Rate of the said several Tolls, Duties, and Sums of Money, so that the Rate of the said respective Tolls, Duties, or Sums of Money, or of any or either of them respectively, shall not be raised or increased beyond the Rate thereof mentioned and specified in this Act, and so that there be always one and the same the same Rate at the same Time for the Ships, Vessels. Lighters, Barges, Boats, Craft, Goods, and Merchandize respectively, from all Persons whatsoever, and whether the said Ships, Vessels. Lighters, Barges, Boats. Craft, Goods, and Merchandize shall enter the said Canal by the said new Entrance at or near the said Place called **Turf or by the said intended Lock so to be made above the said Town of Topsham as aforesaid.**

Appendix 5

**Extracts from the Robert Davy Case v. The City of Exeter,
under the Title of** *The King v. the Mayor, Bailiffs and Commonalty of Exeter,*
as reported at length under the Court's decision dated 11th February 1829.

These Extracts deliberately exclude the lengthy references to charges and tolls etc and the argument as to whether the Canal is a public navigable waterway or a private canal in ownership of the Chamber of Exeter. They solely concentrate on what emerged as the need of Topsham Town for a Second Lock to directly serve its Quay because Robert Davy was not challenging the existence of the Turf Lock, nor the Extension to Turf generally. Please note that all highlights, emphases and underlining are my own and reflect my comments based on my own legal experience over 65 years.

[Case Papers for the Chamber, held at DHC under Ref: Box 21, Location G3/5/5/6 – including the full manuscript of all Pleadings & the Judgment]

Western Times – Saturday 21 February 1829

<u>Court of King's Bench, - Feb. 11, 1829.</u>

<u>The King, v. the Mayor, Bailiffs, and Commonality of Exeter.</u>

Sir James Scarlett. – In the case the King against the Mayor of Exeter, the Solicitor-General is to shew cause why a Mandamus should not be granted.

The Solicitor General. – I am sorry, so near the end of Term, and so near the end of the day, to begin a case that is likely to occupy a considerable time. I really do not see why this case should be pressed so very much, because, even if your Lordships should grant a Mandamus, still the return cannot be till next Term, and it cannot be tried before the Summer Assizes, I submit, therefore, that it might be allowed to stand over for the present.

Sir James Scarlett. – My only reason for pressing it is, that the parties have urged me very much to bring it on as soon as possible; but if your Lordships think that it ought to stand over, till the next term, I have no objection to it.

Lord Tenterden, C.J. – Perhaps if only one counsel were heard upon each side, it might not occupy very long. Will it take up a whole day?

Sir James Scarlett. – Oh dear, no. The great difficulty is to get the gentlemen on both sides together, for when an opportunity presents itself, my learned friend is not always in the way.

Lord Tenterden, C.J. – I do not know how we could fix a day next term, we had better hear the Solicitor General now, for every term brings its own business along with it.

Solicitor General. – I should be very sorry to be heard alone in this case, for it is a local case, and one of very considerable importance to the parties; I trust therefore that your Lordships will hear my friend who is with me.

Lord Tenterden. – We have no objection to hear any gentleman on the same side, but we only hope that we shall not hear the same sentiments from the lips of more than one.

Solicitor General. – This is a rule obtained by Sir James Scarlett, calling upon the Mayor, Bailiffs and Commonality of the City of Exeter, to shew cause why a writ of mandamus should not issue, directed to them, commanding them to open the old and accustomed entrance to the canal, leading from a place called the Lower Sluice, in the river Exe, above the Town of Topsham, to another part of the said river, adjoining the city of Exeter, to replace the lock of the said canal at the said old entrance, and to allow ships to pass and repass through the said old entrance, at the place called the Lower Sluice, and through the said canal to and from the city of Exeter, on payment of the same tolls as have been heretofore paid.

My lords, the grounds upon which this Application was made, appears to have been an affidavit, made by certain persons, five in number, who are resident at Topsham, and who complain that in consequence of an alteration made in the mouth of the navigable canal, which before opened from the river Exe, and communicated with the city of Exeter, by digging a new canal, so as to open into the river Exe two miles lower down than the old entrance, a great part of the profits derived by them as residents of Topsham has been avoided.

For the purpose of supporting this Rule, I understand that they mean to state that this was an old navigable canal, upon which the corporation of the city of Exeter could claim nothing but a certain toll, and they desire that by a mandamus, you will compel the corporation to shut up the new mouth, which they have made, and re-open the ancient sluice. There are two distinct grounds which I mean to bring before this court, in order to shew that I think your Lordships will not interfere in this instance, at all events, by any such proceedings as the issuing of a mandamus. In the first place, I shall be able,

I think satisfactorily, to shew you that this is claimed by the City of Exeter as a canal passing through their own private lands, and the ancient toll that was made having been from time to time varied, I submit that there is not a sufficient ground made to show that this is a public canal, so as to induce you to interfere by this mode of proceeding. But if there were any doubt upon the question, still as there is a much more satisfactory mode of ascertaining the fact, namely by indictment, I submit that you would leave them to their right to the common law mode of trying the fact.

Lord Tenterden, C.J. – Is the canal made under an Act of Parliament?

Solicitor General. – We deny that it is made under an Act of Parliament. - The only authority cited in support of the mandamus when the rule was obtained, is the case of the *King against the Severn and Wye Railway Company* - in this case the Railway was made under the authority of an Act of Parliament ... *(he then proceeded with some technical issues relating to indictments and procedures under an Act of Parliament).*

What I have to say, I will put into the two grounds I have opened; first, there is a great benefit derived to the public in general from this alteration, and no real injury to the people of Topsham; and secondly, I say that this canal is not a public highway, as stated in their affidavits, but it is private right belonging to the corporation. Perhaps it will be more convenient if I take the latter branch of my argument first, because if it should clearly appear that there is no ground upon which to contend that this is a public river or canal, upon which everybody has a right to sail his vessel where he pleases, then, the whole question must fail, for, if the canal be the private right of the corporation, then there can be no possible pretence to say, that they may not alter it as they please. In the first place I may observe, that there is no affidavit made, except by these persons which state that it is a public navigable canal. They say that they believe it to have been, for centuries past, a public navigable canal, for the repairs of which the corporation of Exeter are liable, and for which the corporation had a right to demand the toll of 5s. for each ship. This is the way in which they state the right of the public.

Now, I shall be able to show your Lordships, and I hope satisfactorily, that the canal in question, in the state in which it was before the alteration was made, of which the Topsham people complain, reached from the city of Exeter, first to a place called the Double Lock, where it was communicable with the river Exe, and, in more modern time, it was lengthened to a place called the Lower Sluice, which communicated with the river half a mile above the town of Topsham. The alteration complained of, is the extension, or, if I may so call it, the prolongation of the canal, from the Lower Sluice down to a place called Turf, the stopping up of the Lower Sluice, and making the mouth of the canal open into the river a mile lower down than Topsham.

Lord Tenterden, C.J. - The bend of the river is the point, I suppose?

Sir James Scarlett. - We do not complain that you have made another mouth to the canal. What we complain of is, that you have stopped up the communication between the two places, so as to oblige the people of Topsham to go down the river, and come up again in order to get to Exeter. <u>We say that both may subsist together.</u>

Solicitor General. - I do not know how that may be as to both subsisting together; I don't think they can, but at all events, we say we are not compellable to open it by this mandamus. I am about to shew from the Affidavits, circumstances from which I think the canal may be fairly presumed to be private property. *(Query: Why could both Locks not subsist together? Later in the Case the S-G reverses his position and states that they <u>could</u>!)*

Bayley, J. - Have you stopped up that which was an old navigable canal? Can the people get from Topsham to Exeter without coming by your canal?

Solicitor General. - No, my Lord, they cannot get to Exeter, without coming by our canal; neither could they ever do so. There is a place called the Countess Wear, which has been a perpetual barrier. It has existed ever since the reign of Edward the First. I say, my Lords, that if it appear that the sum of 5s. which they set up to be a constant payment made for every vessel entering the canal, is not a constant payment, but if, from time to time that payment has been altered and varied at the will of the Corporation, then it follows, that it is not a Public navigable River, because it is impossible that any Corporation can have a right of imposing a toll, *ad libitum*[8], over that which is a public highway.

Lord Tenterden, C.J. – The date of the old Canal is not known, is it?

Solicitor General. - It was made about the time of Queen Elizabeth, one part of it at least. I will state to the court a variety of purchases that were made by the Corporation of those very portions of land through which the upper part of the canal passed.

> .....*(here then follows a very lengthy pleading, with comments from the Bench with references to the Affidavits filed, of the succession of deeds for purchasing the land acquisitions for the canal, the silence of the 1539 Act in declaring the canal a public navigable canal (irrelevant because it had not been cut in 1539!) and the question of tolls and the power of taking any tolls at all and with long sections upon the history of tolls and whether them being a uniform toll for a public canal, or not in the case of a private canal)....*

...Now, I say, my Lords, that this is a dealing with the canal, and a mode of conducting themselves in regard to it, which altogether strip it of the

---

[8] *Without restriction*

character of a public navigable canal, and I submit, therefore, that under these circumstances, that you will not call, upon this corporation, who are standing upon their rights, by any summary process, when there is another and far preferable mode of settling the question, namely, by indictment. These are the points with which I mean to trouble you upon this head. Then as to the question of the utility of this alteration, I never in the whole course of my practice saw a case in which utility was more clearly made out.

Lord Tenterden C.J. – They concede that to you, as I understand it; they say that it may be very beneficial to the public at large to have a new line of canal, but **let us have both, is what they want**, at least, so I understood Sir James Scarlett.

Solicitor General. – I do not mean to say that it is impossible to have both, *(n.b. but see his earlier view)* but it is impossible to open the old sluice, because the level of the water is different. But the whole secret of the case consists in one thing; there are no regular Topsham traders, but as the ships could not before conveniently get up to Exeter, the consequence was that vessels of a certain bulk being unable to get up the river, unloaded their cargo at Topsham, and sent it to Exeter partly by lighters, and partly by overland carriage. We state, and it is positively sworn to, that since the alteration of the canal, a vessel from Topsham can get to Exeter by going down the river, and then coming up the canal, in a shorter time than she could before. It was formerly by no means un-frequent for vessels, after having reached the lower part of the canal, to be obliged to wait two or three days, until sufficient water was drawn down from the higher level of the canal, and there was also a constant necessity for discharging the water.

It was moreover necessary to have one pilot to conduct a vessel from the mouth of the river Exe to Topsham, and then to have another pilot from Topsham to navigate a vessel through the canal, *(sic – but surely meaning the Tide-channel/ Back Gut?- no pilotage was required for the canal itself)* but now one pilot carries you from the mouth of the river direct up to the city, and now you may go up the river, unload, take in your cargo, and get out to sea, in less time than a vessel could formerly get up to Exeter. I do assure you, my Lords, that upon the affidavits, as to the utility of this measure there cannot be two opinions upon the subject. The sum of £30,000 has been laid out by the corporation in this undertaking, and it would be extremely hard upon them, unless they were violating a public right, that they should be compelled by this unusual method of proceeding, to strip themselves of all the advantages which they have obtained for their city. It cannot be denied that this application is not an application made for the benefit of the public in general, but it is an application made for the benefit of the Topsham lightermen in particular; but still, I admit that this would not vary the right, if it be a public navigable canal, but I say that it is not so, it is not a canal made under a Public Act of Parliament, for the effect of that Act was only to clear the stream of the river Exe. I say that it is a canal made at the individual expence of the City, which is evidenced by the varying of the tolls from time to time, and it also passes through the very land purchased by the Corporation. Under these circumstances I trust that your Lordships will discharge this Rule, and as to opening the old mouth of the navigable canal, if the Topsham traders are dissatisfied, there is plenty of time for them to prefer an Indictment before the Exeter Assizes, if they please to do so, and if there it should turn out to be a public nuisance, it may be stopped at once.

Mr. Coleridge. – My lords, I am on the same side with the Solicitor-General, and will endeavour as far as possible, to comply with the suggestion thrown out by the court, and will not waste your time with repetitions of that which has already been stated, but as this is a very important case – very important, not to Exeter alone, but also to every other city connected with trade – I trust that I may be indulged with a few observations. If the Rule moved for by Sir James Scarlett be successful, I will venture to say that it will destroy one of the most beneficial public works that has been carried into effect for many years. If your lordships were once in possession of the facts of this case, I think two points will appear beyond all dispute. First, I submit that there is no specific legal right on the part of the applicants; and secondly, that there is no want of a complete remedy by other means.

Lord Tenterden. – You mean to say the remedy might have been by indictment?

Mr. Coleridge. – Yes, my Lord, but if we should fail on these points, I should then shew that the grievances which are alleged as the foundation of the Rule are most completely answered. Now it appears from the affidavits made on both sides, that there are ancient weirs and bridges upon the river Exe, which prevented it being a navigable river before the reign of Henry the 8th, in which reign an Act of Parliament was passed, which, after reciting the antiquity of the usage, states that ships, boats, and vessels had had from their course and recourse in the river Exe, to and from the high seas, but that this had for a long time been destroyed. These words are important, it is alleged that the navigable channel of the river Exe

> "had a long time been so destroyed and letted by weirs and drivings of sand and gravel by course of the water into the said river, and other letts and nuisances, that at this day, and a long time past, ships, boats and vessels, have not had, nor yet can have, their course to and from our said city, as of old time they have had, by reason whereof your said supplicants a long time have been, and yet be compelled and enforced to carry their goods and merchandize from the ships, boats, and vessels to our said city by land." Then comes the enacting words, "that it may and shall be lawful at all times after the Feast of Easter now next coming, to our said supplicants, Mayor, Bailiffs

and Commonality of our said city of Exeter, and your successors to pluck down, dig, mine, break, bank, and cast up, all and manner of weirs, locks, sand, gravels and other letts and nuisances whatsoever they be, in the said River, and in other places and grounds convenient and necessary for the same wheresoever they be, lying between our said city upon the high sea."

Lord Tenterden. - What Act is that?

Mr. Coleridge. – It is a private (*n.b. this is wrong – the published Act is headed as being an "Acte Publicke"*) Act of Parliament of the 31st of Henry the 8th. This Act of Parliament undoubtedly gives them no powers to make a canal - the grievances complained of are hindrances in the channel of the River, and the permission given is a permission to remove those grievances. If it be necessary to purchase lands here, undoubtedly a power is given them so to do, and a specific mode of payment is pointed out, namely, a recomence *(i.e. a valuation)* to be determined by the Justices of Assize for the time being. It appears that nothing was done under this Act of Parliament in that reign, but in the 9th year of the reign of Queen Elizabeth, the Corporation had found that the Countess's Weir and the bridges could not be removed, and it then seems that they first thought of making a canal. The antiquity of the obstruction in the river is proved by the very name of Countess Weir, which derived its appellation from one of the Courtney family, a Countess of Devon, who was supposed to have put the weir there. In the 9th year of the reign of Queen Elizabeth, as is proved by deeds which we have here (and in no one of which there is the least reference to this Act of Parliament) they purchased the lands extending between the city of Exeter down to just below the Countess Weir; if your lordships will look at the plan which you have, you will see that a little below the Countess Weir the canal comes very close to the channel of the river, and it's sworn by the Chamberlain of the city, who has taken these plans and examined the spots, and he has reason to believe from the appearance of the place, that the original channel of the canal was carried into the river just below the countess Weir. So, the canal stood at the time, and so it continued till the reign of William the 3rd. Then our affidavits state that there was a petition presented to the House of Commons, stating that the Mayor and Chamber of the city of Exeter had expended many thousand pounds in enlarging the canal, and were unable to go on for want of money and praying for a Bill to grant them the power of levying a rate for the purpose. This was in 1695, and this petition was met by a counter petition on the part of the inhabitants of Exeter, and the result was no Bill passed; an order of the chamber was then made, that as soon as money could be raised the works should go on, for they were then suspended for want of money. It was at that period that the latter part of the canal was added *(i.e. by extension from Matford Brook down to the Lower Sluice, originally named Trenchard's Sluice, in about 1699/1701)* and it is for the stopping up that entrance so made in the reign of William the 3rd, long after the first making of the canal, and long after the passing of the Act of Henry the 8th, and no other Act ever passed upon the subject - it is for stopping up that entrance so circumstanced that these proceedings are now taken, and the present application is made. This brought the canal into the river Exe a considerable way above the town of Topsham; but the way in which it was made was by the most inartificial mode imaginable. It was not formed by a lock, but there was only a pair of gates, the consequence of which was that when a ship or boat came in or went out it was necessary to lead off the water until you brought it to a level with the river below. Besides this there was a brook which was called the Alphington brook.

Lord Tenterden. Was this in the time of King William? *(n.b. this was about 1699/1701 under Daniel Dunnell's Improvements).*

Mr. Coleridge. - Yes, and it emptied itself into the new canal, and in consequence of this it is sworn that the level at the double lock was four feet higher than the level at the lower sluice. At the entrance of every vessel, it was necessary to let down the water from the higher level of the canal, in order to enable a vessel to pass the lower sluice, and this was a mile and three quarters in length, with an average breadth of from fifty to sixty feet. When you had got out of the 'channel' *(sic – but surely 'Canal'?)* into the lower sluice, you got into what is sworn to be a very intricate narrow channel *(the Tide-channel/ Back Gut, I suggest)* and in fact it was always necessary to take a separate pilot from Topsham for the navigation of the 'canal' *(sic – but again, surely 'Channel'; i.e. the Tide-channel/ Back Gut?)* , from there *(i.e. Topsham?)* through to the lower sluice, in addition to the one you had to take on board at the entrance of the river. *(i.e. at the Exmouth Bar?)* In the course of this passage *(i.e. through the Tide-channel/ Back Gut)* there is a shoal, and between Topsham and the point where the *(now extended?)* 'canal' goes into the 'sea', *(sic – but might this mean the navigable channel between Topsham and the Entrance of the extended Canal at Turf Pool where there is such a shoal?)* – there was another shoal *(query: the Black Oar Bank)*; the consequence of which was, that many vessels that could pass the Bar at Exmouth, could not get to Topsham, but even if the vessel could get up to Topsham, she was obliged to lay there for several tides before she could pass up the river. The consequence was that vessels destined originally for the Exeter Trade, could not take in their loading at Exeter, but the goods were brought in lighters to Topsham.

Lord Tenterden. – Of that we have been informed by the Solicitor General. *[i.e. a subtle hint to stop repetition!]*

Mr. Coleridge. – There was also a considerable land carriage from Topsham to Exeter, which had grown up – but however, this is not stated in the affidavits as the ground of the injury of which they complain, but their complaint is the injury to the coasting trade. This injury is stated by one coasting trader, &

we have affidavits made, by I know not how many coasting traders, distinctly negativing the assertion; and this, I submit is not immaterial to the point. My position is, that it is clear, that this was not an immemorial highway. It commenced in the reign of Queen Elizabeth. It could not be created a highway under the Act of Parliament of Henry the 8th, because that Act gave no power to make a canal, nor any power to levy a toll, and it is incredible that it could direct a canal to be made without also levying a Toll......
... (*there then followed a lengthy submission regarding tolls which is not directly related to the issues in my Argument*) ... So much then for the want of legal right, in this case, on the part of the applicants, but I say, that if they have a legal right, they have also a distinct legal remedy. Suppose an Indictment were preferred and found, and that they succeeded in proving a continual nuisance, the effect of that indictment would be to compel an abatement of the nuisance, for there are cases in the 8th Term Reports, and also a Case in the 1st, *Strange, of the King v. Tullamore*, which settled this point. Now it is sworn that if these sluices were put down, and the lock were to be opened and shut as before, the canal could not exist, and this does not stand upon speculation. Green and Telford have made their own Report upon this subject, and Mr. Green has stated all the circumstances, he states that the consequence of the constant emptying of the canal, and the flux and reflux of the water, the sides were always falling in, and that it is absolutely necessary to the existence of the canal, that a new principle should be adopted for the purpose of converting it into a permanent floating basin. But if you say that we should restore the old sluice in its former state, you are saying that the canal must be emptied every time.

Lord Tenterden. – You say the canal is always full?

Mr Coleridge. Yes, it is never emptied now at all, as there is a sea lock. The benefit of this is, that any vessel which can pass the Bar at Exmouth, can with the same tide reach the quay at Exeter, she comes there from the sea lock, and horses being put to her she gets up at once. But, then, my friends will say that if we had this judgment and abatement, we should not be so foolish as to comply in terms with their Rule, but that we should put up a proper lock. That would be their answer. Now, the reply to that answer is this – that if the lock were put up, the state of the level would be such that it would be stopped up by the constant rushing of the water, and my friends would lose all the benefit of their proceedings, for there would be an end of the canal altogether. Take it in wither way, if there were an Indictment, the right must be to abate the nuisance, they would get all the benefit they desire by the destruction of our canal and lock, although the effect might be to stop the channel below. They may obtain an abatement of the nuisance, that would be all, there is nothing that this mandamus can give them more than an Indictment can do. It may be said that an Indictment will not lay against the corporation however that may be, at all events they could easily Indict any individual who had put up the obstruction. Now these are the principal points upon which I rely. With regard to the other points, I say they are distinctly answered with respect to the general merits of the case, and distinctly answered as to the general benefit arising from this undertaking. I would beg my leave to say here, that as my Lord Chief Justice has remarked this day, how numerous have been lately the applications for *Quo Warranto Informations, (i.e. A Writ of Right in the King's Bench for the Crown against someone making a claim or who usurps an office, franchise or liberty, to enquire by* **what authority** *he supports his claim in order to determine the right).* I think I may say that the applications for mandamus have been still more frequent, and perhaps still more prejudicial. I may say that it is not even the absence of a complete remedy which will induce the court to interfere. Several cases may be found in which the court have refused to grant a mandamus where an Indictment would lie, although it might not give the full remedy. It was refused in one instance to grant a mandamus for payment of some money which had been taken as damages at the Sessions, although an Indictment would not there afford a perfect remedy. In these cases, your Lordships will, I am sure, always look whether there is any public benefit resulting from the application. I think in this case I may say, that they have failed in shewing any specific legal right, they only state that the river Exe is not navigable except by means of this canal for which they have to pay a certain toll. When they have not stated their legal right, I think it will be going rather too far, for the court to presume that in their favour.

Sir James Scarlett. – My friends seem to understand something of the general principle on which I moved this Rule, but neither of them have touched the exact grounds on which I obtained it – however, they appear to contend against the principle on which I made the original Motion. When your lordships come to look at the statute of Henry the 8th, you will see that by that statute **the corporation of Exeter were bound to render the river Exe a navigable river and if they have made substitution instead of doing so, I ask how could that substitution be for their private benefit? If they made a substitution for the river which they were bound to render navigable, they must leave the substitution instead of what they took away.** They state in their petition on which the Act is founded, that in former times the river Exe was navigable from the sea, up to the port of Exeter but that for a long time past this navigation had been stopped by reason of certain weirs, and the driving of the sand, and that consequently they have been obliged to carry their goods by land instead of water, to their great loss and inconvenience. Then they pray of the Crown *"that it may and shall lawful at all times after the Feast of Easter, now next coming, to your said suppliants Mayors, Bailiffs, and Commonality of your said city of Exeter, and their successors, to pluck down, dig, mine, break, bank, and cast up and all manner of weirs, rocks, sands, gravels, and other letts and nuisances whatsoever they be, in the said river, and in other places and ground convenient* *and necessary for the same, whosesoever they be, lying between your said city and the high sea. And further, to do and make other things requisite and necessary, whereby the said ships, boats, and vessels may have their sure course and recourse in the said river, to and from your said city, and there to charge and discharge the said goods and merchandizes without let or disturbance of any person or person giving and paying therefore unto the lord or lords, owner or owners of the soil where such digging and mining shall be, in recompense and satisfaction of and for the land or ground so to be digged and mined, after the rate of 20 years purchase, or else as much for the same as shall be adjudged, ordained, determined by the King's Justices of Assize, in the County of Devon, for the time being."* Here, then, is the Act of Parliament, my friends say that they have not proceeded to act under that statute, because they did not pluck down the weirs as they might have done. I admit that they did not proceed under the act, to its full extent, because they probably found it more convenient to make a canal, than to do what was there directed but I will tell your Lordships what they did do. It appears, by their own affidavits, that they built a weir across the river. They were authorized, by this Act, to pull down weirs; the only ancient weir which existed between Topsham and Exeter, they were authorized to pull down, but instead of that they thought fit to build up another. *[i.e. Trew's Weir 1663].* They shew, by their books and affidavits, that they contemplated the pulling down of the first weir, but afterwards, changing their minds, we find them buying lands, and making a canal, and they then built another weir, which makes it impossible for the vessels to navigate the whole of the river. What I contend is this, that **they have substituted this canal, which existed in the reign of King William, for the river**. I contend that they have made this substitution; but if they had been content to have exacted a reasonable toll, the public would not have objected to it. As to the variation of the toll, which has been insisted upon so much by my friends, all they shew is, that they have received the toll; but it is evident that they have confounded in the extracts, which they have given us from their books, the entries relating to the charges for landing goods, and for their claim to wharfage, and the use of the quay, which is quite different from the toll of a canal. I will give my friends the advantage they can get from the circumstance of the variation of the toll. The charge was once five shillings for every ship, and two shillings and six-pence for every ton of the goods which she contained. They have the affidavit of the Wharfinger, who has found among his books that in 1715 there was an entry that a ship was to pass for 5s. the charge for plankage being 6d. and this continued down to 1754, when they remitted the plankage, and the sum of 5s.6d. was the uniform charge upon each ship; the same toll with this single variation has prevailed from the year 1715 down to this day. The entries before that time are very ambiguous, they are either entries of remittances of tolls to some particular individuals, or entries of some particular tolls & charges for landing goods at Exeter quay. We do not deny in our affidavits, that the canal recently opened, may be useful to the public in certain particulars, and in certain places; but it is sufficient for us to say, that a portion of the public who were accustomed to navigate the ancient canal, are prejudiced by the removal of the entrance of the canal into the river. *(i.e. at the Lower Sluice and then via the Tide-channel/ Back Gut).*

This is a tide river, and the tide flows through the lower sluice towards Exeter; they take advantage of this tide and fill their canal by taking the water out of the river. It is sworn to by one or two persons, not navigators, but inhabitants of Exeter, that it was the practice of many vessels to go direct from London to Topsham and land a part of their goods there, and then go from Topsham to Exeter, and all this inconvenience is now raised that they must first go up the river to Topsham, then down, and come again in order to come to Exeter.

Those vessels are subject to the same difficulty and inconvenience in regard to pilotage, which was pointed out as having existed before, as they must still go up to that part of the river which requires pilotage; and then, when they come to Topsham, they must go down again. They must pay 5s. for the vessel, and 6d. per ton besides, so that a vessel of seventy-two tons would have to pay thirty-six shillings.

Mr. Coleridge. – With regard to the present rate of tolls, I may state that it is experimental, and not meant to be continued.

Sir James Scarlett. – This right which they insist upon, may be a most disastrous one, for according to that they may say that they will exclude us altogether, and entirely stop up the navigation to the port of Exeter. What I say is, that when it appears that for a great number of years, perhaps for 120 years, a **dedication** is made to the public of the channel of a navigable river upon payment of a certain toll, it is too much for them in such a case to have the power of excluding the Public, or compelling them to be at a greater expence for the purpose of putting a large profit into the pockets of the corporation.

Topsham is a populous and increasing town, it is within a short distance of Exeter, and carries on a considerable trade; and there is no reason why their whole trade should be sacrificed, that vessels may go past them to Exeter, instead of stopping at Topsham in transition to Exeter.

Now, my Lords, in speaking upon the subject of this mandamus, my friend, Mr. Coleridge, has furnished me with the best possible reason to shew why a mandamus is the best possible remedy in this case, as according to him, the effect of an Indictment, would only be an abatement of the nuisance, which could not answer the purpose in this case but your Lordships, by your jurisdiction a writ of mandamus, would take care that the purpose was answered, and that they should effectually do that which really would be beneficial to the public. If in consequence of what they have done, the opening of the gates should be attended with some prejudice to the navigation, it behoves them to set it right in the best manner that it can be done; they might do it by a lock. We are not such fools as to ask a thing to be done which would be of no use to us; but my friends say, however the facts may be, they ought to be tried by a jury. An Indictment has all the objections that present themselves in the case which the Solicitor General handed up to your lordships, and which was alluded to by me in moving for the Rule; where, upon consideration, it was held by the court that it did not follow, because the grievance complained of might happen to be a public nuisance, that therefore a mandamus could not be applied for. But above all cases a mandamus should be applied for in the present instance, because in this particular case, they contend for a private right. It appears to me, that this corporation of Exeter, do not very well consult their own interests, because, by raising the tolls they raise a question with the public as to the right to do that which they have done, the effect may be, that they may put their whole property into jeopardy by taking these tolls. The public are content to pay that toll, which the current custom of a hundred years has sanctioned; but I do not know that they will submit to pay this new imposition. But it may be said, that the party may bring action against the corporation, – so he may, but that is not a specific remedy to obtain the removal of an evil. I do not agree with what Mr. Coleridge has said as to the granting of writs of mandamus being productive of harm, I humbly conceive that a writ of mandamus is highly useful in many instances, and **far better than to have recourse to a Bill in Chancery.** *(n.b. enough said)* It may be quite true that the applications for such writs are more frequent than usual – the avocations of mankind are multiplied – their dealings are increased, and far more intricate, and this gives rise to the frequent applications for writs of mandamus. It a very cheap mode, and at the same time a very efficacious one of obtaining a remedy, and I am persuaded that the difficulty of procuring a writ of mandamus in ancient times, very much induced the practice of so many persons to have recourse to Chancery. I am sure that there is no objection on the part of this court to give expences to its suitors, and if it should appear, that any one of the King's subjects can be spared **the expence of a suit in Equity**, *[n.b. once again!]* this court will not hesitate to issue a writ of mandamus by its own proper jurisdiction. I trust upon the whole your Lordships will think it right that this Rule should be made absolute.

Mr. Follett. – My lords, I am on the same side with Sir James Scarlett. This is a case of great public importance, because the defence goes to the full extent of saying that the whole trade of the port of Exeter, which has by far the greatest trade in that part of the country, entirely to be dependent upon the will and pleasure of the individuals composing the corporation, and that not remotely, but directly; because my friends contend that they have a right to stop up immediately, if they choose, the only possible means by which vessels can get to the city of Exeter from the sea. That is the nature of their claim, and that is the nature the argument used by their Counsel, although it appears both from our and their own affidavits, that this canal has been for centuries past, the only means of getting ships up to Exeter. Now, if your Lordships be satisfied that there has been public navigation for centuries past, and that the public are entitled to use this navigation, then all the arguments used by my friends to shew this new canal of so much convenience, will be of no avail; for then they would have no right to do this, except by permission of an act of Parliament. We do not, however, say that this canal is not more useful than the former one, though perhaps we might be justified in saying so, **all we say is, let the old entrance be replaced, leave your new entrance, and let the public choose for themselves; let it be said, "here is the canal - here are the two ways to get to Topsham, and let the public choose which they like best." It is quite possible to have both the entrances, and my friends know it is quite possible,** for although they have the evidence of several engineers, yet there is not one of them that will venture to swear that the two entrances could not exist together, - they will not swear it because they know they could, – they might have the two entrances to this canal one above and one below the town of Topsham. But, in addition to extending this canal, they have done still more, for they have raised the toll twenty-fold. If they have a right to do this, they have a right to say "you shall not pass without paying two pounds for each ship," and then they would have obstructed the navigation of the canal to Exeter, and shut up the port, by this toll which was never paid before. They have done so, to a certain extent, by this additional toll, and this is above all other cases, one that is particularly fit for writ of mandamus; it is just such a case as that referred to by James Scarlett and the grounds upon which I ask for it are, that an Indictment for an action is not a complete and proper way obtaining redress, - here there is no remedy so effectual as a mandamus, **particularly where one of the parties concerned is a corporation.** *(n.b. My suggestion that this is the precursor of the modern Application for a Judicial Review against Government decisions or other Authority).* Now it has been said by Mr. Coleridge, that this is not an immemorial highway, – it is not necessary that it should be, if the highway have existed for centuries, it is a highway for all intents and purposes; nor is it at all inconsistent with the fact of its being a highway, or public road, that it should be subject to the payment of toll, because, there are a number of public roads which are subject to the payment of toll.

Mr Coleridge. – (comments in a long section on tolls upon Goods – not upon ships - and upon Book entries for tonnages relevant to them for a public right of passage, with details not relevant to the issues being pleaded by Sir James Scarlett) …

Mr. Follett. – That is as to the toll upon goods; but I am speaking of the toll upon ships; however, they have shewn no variation upon the toll of goods. It is exactly the same from the year 1715 to 1754, and from down to the present time there is variation. I submit, therefore, that looking at all the affidavits on both sides, it is quite clear that, at least for the last century, this has been a public highway, upon the payment of a specific toll. The corporation of Exeter say that it is their own property, and that they have a right to make as much profit out of it as they please; but I submit that they have no such right, and as there is no remedy which the public have to prevent their exercising this unjust power, except a writ of mandamus. I trust that your Lordships will make this Rule absolute. If there be any thing in what my friends have said in their argument, they may give effect to that in their Return to the mandamus.

[The lordships then consulted together for a few minutes]

Lord Tenterden, C.J. – We think upon the whole that the court must discharge this Rule. – The first and principle question is, whether the public have a right to the navigation of this Canal into the River Exe? That is the first question, and that is a question that may be tried by Indictment against the corporation for stopping the entrance – that may be tried by Indictment. The other questions that may follow, may afterwards become fit subjects for the consideration of the court, and if the public right be established, upon the trial of the Indictment, - which is the regular course – if the public right should be so established, and if the interposition of this court is then found requisite to compel the corporation to do that which they ought to do; namely to give the public the full benefit of that which belongs to them; it will then be time for an Application for a Mandamus, but at present we think the Application is premature, as the question should be first tried in the usual manner by Indictment. Rule Discharged.

(Without Costs – *i.e. Each Party had to pay their own Costs*)

Appendix 6

Extracts from the Public Speech of Mayor, Robert Rogers Sanders, as reported by the Exeter and Plymouth Gazette on Saturday 02 October 1830

Navigation of the Exe, opening of the new dock, and Dinner for the Mayor and Corporation on the 29th September 1830 - Extract: -

The Mayor, R. R. Sanders, Esq. rose to return thanks, & spoke nearly as follows. - Mr. Chairman and gentlemen, for the honour you have done the Mayor and Chamber of Exeter, I beg to return you our thanks; but perhaps on such as occasion as the present, something more must be expected from me than merely acknowledging the honour you have done, us; I will therefore, with your permission, go into a brief detail of the circumstances that have arisen during the progress of the work, the near completion of which we are this day met to celebrate; in doing which I promise not to introduce anything that is irrelevant, and I hope not to dwell longer on any point than may be necessary for explanation. It is well-known to all acquainted with the port of Exeter, that the Canal navigation was extremely defective, and stood in need of great repair. It had also the reputation of being an expensive port; but those who understood the question, well knew that that expense arose more from the intricate state of the navigation, and being dependent on the tides, than from any other cause. (Applause) The banks were very much out of repair, and we found that it would cost a very considerable sum of money to put them in an efficient state; a further examination was made, and it was found necessary to extend it; and here let me observe, that the idea of extending the Canal is not a novel one. I have a document in my pocket bearing date about 1690 where there is an estimate for completing the navigation of the Canal, and there is also an estimate for extending the then present lock to a place called Turf - about 2 miles from the entrance of the Canal - at £6000. By this I only mean to show that we take no credit to ourselves for striking out a new idea, but only for carrying into effect what was previously designed by, & which our forefathers wished themselves to have done. (Cheers) Having come to the determination of lengthening the Canal, it became necessary that we should consult those who had land in the neighbourhood, and asking their permission to carry our line through it. On that point I am happy to say we found a very appropriate reception & support (Applause); and I take this opportunity of returning the thanks of the Chamber of Exeter; to the Trustees of Lord Courtenay, Sir L. Palk (who I am happy to see present) Sir J. Acland, & many others, whom, perhaps, I shall mention, before I sit down. **Things went on very well, till a hostile feeling arose in the neighbouring town of Topsham**, which was soon backed by some of our fellow citizens, who from some false impressions with respect to the Chamber, were induced to treat us in a manner which was well calculated to surprise us. But a little time and **a little reflection soon removed the veil from their eyes**, and they have been since **pleased to give us credit for the purity of our motives** - and so convinced were they of it, that the gentleman who took the lead *(n.b.our Robert Davy…)* found that he could no longer keep his committee together. (Hear, and laughter.) Since then, I am happy to say, that gentleman has expressed himself in a far different manner, and upon the present occasion he has said that he would turn his sword into a ploughshare. (Cheers) I have referred to Topsham, and I will take occasion particularly to mention that the **Messrs. Davy's** of that town thought they should receive very considerable injury - they fought us manfully and we fought them, **till a compromise took place satisfactory to both parties**; (cheers) and in mentioning **Mr. Davy**, I beg to say, that from the moment that that compromise took place, no man could have lent his hand more willingly to the Chamber to carry forward what still remained to be done. (Loud Cheering.)!

Appendix 7

Letters to the Western Times (various)

Exeter and Plymouth Gazette – Saturday 22 September 1827
Mr. Trood made a complaint against four of his lightermen, for demanding more wages than they had agreed for, in consequence of the extension of the new Canal having increased their labour. Mr. Trood admitted this fact, and stated that before the completion of the Canal his vessels sailed up to near the lower sluice, but now they had to be towed up the new works, by his men. The Bench considered, that if the men's labour was increased, their wages ought to be advanced; and Mr. Trood concurring in the justice of this decision, the complaint was dismissed.

Western Times – Saturday 20 October 1827
(Just after the Extension had been completed and before Robert Davy's Rule)
To the Editor of the Exeter Weekly Times.

Sir, - Having few remarks to make on the propriety of the Chamber of Exeter extending the line of the Canal should you think them worthy of a place in your impartial paper, you will oblige a constant reader.

It is well known to every man acquainted with the navigation of the river, that as soon as a vessel reaches Turf Perch, (the present entrance of the New Cut) there is plenty of water from thence at any tides to Black Bar Perch at the bottom of Topsham town. The distance from thence to Lower Sluice, the entrance of the Old Canal, is from a half to three quarters of a mile, the bottom of which is a clay mould, screened or land-locked by the town of Topsham, on the eastern-side, and by the Exminster land on the western-side; a great part of which is at present deep water; so that would only have required deepening the soil part of the way. This would have required nothing but manual labour; and it is presumed the deepening of it about 2 Feet would have cost but very little, compared with that of the present cut; which there no question would have answered every necessary purpose, and never wanted any further repairs; for by letting out the waste water that remained after the vessels passed up between the lower lock and double lock, at dead low water, this, in addition to the fresh coming down the old river, would have always scoured the channel and kept it open. The effect of this may be seen by 2 or 3 reservoirs on a very small scale, in the neighbourhood made for that purpose; but this was by far too liberal a plan for the Chamber to think of doing. - No, the old ancient town of Topsham would have benefited by this plan; and that was in decided opposition to the wishes of the Chamber, they would rather have put a chain across the river, to prevent vessels coming up at all, than to add any facility to its trade; but selfish illiberal acts, Mr Editor, often defeat themselves; and if I am not grossly mistaken, the Chamber will soon find themselves like the dog in the fable, who grasped at the shadow and lost the substance.

It must be observed, Mr. Editor, that vessels coming in the old tract, called at Topsham, landed the goods designed for Honiton, Tiverton, Cullumpton, &c. then passed on their way with a flood-tide to the entrance at Lower-lock. They have now, after taking out probably half their cargo, to beat down the worst navigation of the river, to the entrance of the New Canal, which may take them as much time as going from Topsham to London, or London to Topsham.   NAUTICUS.

Western Times – Saturday 24 May 1828 *(Just after the Rule had been granted)*

EXETER LOCAL.

The attention of the inhabitants of Exeter and Topsham, and the neighbourhood, connected with the navigation of Exeter, is at the time directed to the progress of a proceeding last week brought before the Court of King's Bench, at the instance of certain inhabitants of Topsham, and on which the Court granted a Rule Nisi.

Our Exeter readers, from perusing the copy of the rule in another part of our paper, will readily understand the point in question but to our distant friends it may be necessary to state, that for centuries back, the navigation from the High Seas to the City of Exeter has been in front of Topsham to the entrance of the canal, at a place called the lower sluice, and up the ship canal to the city, and the toll was five shillings for every vessel, be the size what it might. - There was some inconvenience between the old mouth of the canal and Topsham but which it is asserted might have been cleared, and the channel deepened, for small annual expense:- But it seems the Chamber of Exeter, in its consummate wisdom, without consulting the public, principally interested in the navigation having thought that such economical improvement of the navigation (before as expensive as any in the kingdom) would not hand down the names of the members to posterity with sufficient *eclat*, determined to cut an extension of the canal for 2 miles, at an expense it is said of 60, or £70,000.

– The tolls on passing through these new works appear to be exorbitant, and for a vessel of 200 tons, upwards of ten times as much as before. – The Chamber, in order to lessen the number of the opponents to the measure, has taken the precaution of laying all the additional toll on the vessels, and none on the cargo, little expecting that the ship owners would contest the point. But it appears that this body has again found itself mistaken in its calculations for the inhabitants of Topsham are in the field. – Most of the coasting vessels unload part of their cargoes at Topsham & the rest at Exeter. The Chamber, calculating on controlling them, have attached the toll on the tonnage of the vessel, and not the cargo, so that, as an instance, a vessel a week or two since unloaded all her cargo as consigned at Topsham, except 3 hogsheads of gin, for Mr. Crockett, one of the Chamber; – the captain of course wished to land that also at Topsham, but Mr. Crockett absolutely made him go down from Topsham to the mouth of the New Canal, about two miles. – Then haul up at a considerable expence, and as the vessel was 100 tons register the captain was obliged to pay £2.10s. If 110 tons £3.15s, besides the additional other expenses, and loss of time, because Mr. Crockett was one of the Chamber, while perhaps the whole freight of the gin from London was not a quarter part of the money. – We suppose any other consignee would have consented that his gin might have been brought from Topsham to Exeter by land.

It is to remedy evils like this, that the prosecutors are, we understand, applying to the Court of King's Bench, to have the old entrance opened, and leave the public to elect which passage for their advantage. – If the new works be really an improvement, the public are not too blind to perceive it, and will crowd into the new canal; but they are attached to the wisdom of our forefathers, who formed the old entrance, subject to the old tolls, they hope to have the power of using it.

These Corporation jobs, as they are called, require good looking after. – It is a nuisance indeed, that a small majority of a corporate body, should have in its power the managing and controlling the commercial interests of this city and neighbourhood – We shall anxiously wait, the argument on the rule, - we are enabled to give in another column a copy of the Rule Nisi, and hope to give a report at length when the defendants show cause in the next term.

Western Times – Saturday 11 October 1828 *(Just as the Consent Order was granted for the Hearing in February 1829)*

EXETER LOCAL - THE CANAL.

The cessation of intercourse between the city and the sea, which has again taken place, recalls our attention to this subject, replete as is with interest to the commercial and consuming parts of this neighbourhood. We understand that foundations are laying down for a lock, to communicate with what is called a basin, or floating dock, into which we suppose eventually, ever completed, all vessels will be compelled to go, and subject to fresh charges for dock dues, &c. and the wharfs adjoining being on the land of the Chamber, will be subject to all sorts of charges, and that the bonded and other cellars lately built near the present quay will be rendered useless, to make way for others to be built near the new dock, on the land of the Chamber. We have been amused, it is true, by report of a bridge to be thrown across the river, and have heard of building castles in the air; - the expence alone would be a bar to the measure. The inconvenience the trade of Exeter will suffer, by the wharf being so far removed from the city, well deserves the consideration of the inhabitants. When we see these public works, of our corporation, we always look for some interest to be served, as to the property of some leading individuals of the body, to their corporate property, to be applied to their "general purposes." We could refer to a late work, but reserve that for a future occasion.

We have recently received a very curious document, shewing the income of the corporation from this canal for a series of years and from the source from which it comes, we have no doubt of its correctness. It is complete, except to one item. We shall endeavour to fill that blank, and then give the document to the public. We shall be obliged to any gentleman to give us any information on the subject, as we wish to make it as full and correct as possible; for as the members of that body will keep hidden from the public, the information they ought to make public, we must get it at the best way we can. We have a good groundwork, but shall be glad of any information to compare with it. On this subject we must give our readers a general result, which we think may, in round numbers, be depended on: that after paying the expence of repairs and management, the revenue of the canal, on the old tolls, produced about £3,000 per annum. Lord Rolle's interest was perhaps leaving £2,000 per annum net income.

In order to support the argument, we intend to urge, we will suppose a man to keep a public house, and to make an annual profit. At the end of 30 years, this house wants repair or improvements, for the better accommodation of his guests, what would be that of that man, who should say to his friends, I must charge you a heavier price of the goods you buy of me, in order to enable me to make these alterations? They would laugh at him for a blockhead, and particularly if a large portion of his customers should think the alterations would be no improvement.

We must not call our corporation such a name, but we think the adding to the toll on the shipping in passing our canal would justify those interested in the navigation in expressing themselves very strongly on the subject. For if the canal has netted the corporation £2,000, per annum, and the members of that body, in their collective wisdom, have for some time past felt for the public a sympathy for any inconvenience in the approach to the city, the course to have been pursued should have been, to have funded that surplus income until it had, by accumulation and compound interest, amounted to the sum required, and thus have discharged their duty as faithful stewards of the public purse. – But for centuries back, the profits of this navigation have been applied by the chamber to their "general purposes," nobody knows how, no public account of its application appearing, the conjectures of the inhabitants have been left at sea, to suppose what they please, with nothing to rest on but to wonder why men of business, whose time must be of value to them, should be anxious to fill public offices which must necessarily occupy so much of their time. – It is a secret which no one has been able to fathom.

Suppose this £2,000, per annum had been economised for 30 years: with compound interest, it would have amounted to a much larger sum than has been required for the late alterations and the trade need not have been charged with the enormous heavy additional tolls with which it is now encumbered. – If these alterations be an improvement to the navigation, they might have been completed to the public advantage; but we deny that the trade is generally benefitted. - A vessel now and then may be expedited, (of which Mr. Woolmer takes care to let us know,) but considering the enormous increase of tolls, we say the advantage is not commensurate; while we are prepared to shew that the whole advantage might have been gained, by cleansing the old channel, for five thousand pounds. – An attempt has been made to ruin the trade of Topsham, but that will be settled next term.

We call on the citizens of Exeter to attend to this matter. – If they will remain passive, and let that body, who ought to protect their interests, trample on their rights, and tax them at pleasure, and without control, (for if they can support the present increased tolls, they may multiply them to an unlimited extent) they may do so, but it is when the evil is fresh, they are called on to combat it, and before time has given it an implied sanction. – We believe the present increase of toll will amount to at least £1,000, per annum. – This is a tax on the inhabitants. – If this be submitted to, we know that double that sum, or even more may be added, when time has some degree given colour to the right of increasing the tolls at all; and so on, until the expences of the port, bad as they now are, may become the ruin of the trade altogether.

Fellow citizens, – this matter deserves your serious attention.

Western Times - Saturday 27 December 1828 *(Awaiting the Hearing on 11th February 1829)*

To the Editor of the Exeter Weekly Times.

SIR – Having been called on, in a letter signed "an inhabitant of Exeter," in the *Exeter Flying Post*, to answer certain interrogatories put by him, relating to the new Canal; I do so, for the same reasons he has himself given for putting them, namely, for the purpose of preventing many persons being misled, who do not understand the subject.

Without answering all this inhabitant's interrogatories, I will, in my turn, beg to ask him, what could possibly have induced the inhabitants of Topsham, of every distinction, to shew hostility to the extension of the Canal, if they were not convinced that their own interests were to be injured by it. I presume it is hardly necessary for me to tell this gentleman that all person in trade are actuated solely by their own interests; and that, as long as human nature is constituted as we find it, this principle will invariably guide and control their actions: and, I have no doubt, but that the close connection of this inhabitant of Exeter with the guildhall, and its emoluments, have influenced him to give so much candid advice to the inhabitants of Topsham from precisely the same motives.

This gentleman boldly asserts, that the inhabitants of Topsham, instead of being injured in any manner by this new Canal, will really be benefitted by it; and that they ought to follow his advice, and submit to lose the navigation the upwards from their town, because he is friendly enough to tell them so. But the gentleman must be told that the inhabitants of Topsham do not require his advice; they are perfectly aware what their rights are, and are determined to protect them by all the means which the laws of their country admit of.

Now Sir, what is really the gist of the case. All goods brought into this port have, been hitherto discharged, either at Exmouth or Topsham, and conveyed from these places to Exeter in barges, lighters, &c, or the vessels have proceeded onwards, as was found most convenient to the shippers, or the masters of the vessels, by the old canal, on paying five shillings for each vessel and certain dues on the goods, established from time immemorial. It is now endeavoured to increase the dues to ten times the former amount, on vessels, barges, &c, and to impose certain higher tolls on all goods; and, besides, to compel ships and barges, of all descriptions, instead of passing upwards and following the course of the river from Topsham, to return again down the river to Turf, to enter the new Canal. What these additional tolls may be, rests at Present in the breasts of the Chamber.

It has been stated by an Editor of an Exeter Paper, connected with the Chamber, and, I believe, who forms a part of it, that nearly £100,000, will have been expended on this undertaking. If this be correct, surely the importers of Exeter cannot look at the expenditure of such a sum, however plausible may the declaration of its managers, that it has been done solely for their advantage, without the most serious alarm and apprehension for their trade, coupled with their notice for an act of the legislature to legalise it. It will not be enough for them to be told that they will all fare alike under their new impositions, and consequently that no competition will exist amongst themselves. The citizens of Exeter have too much sense not to know that they are bound to look for competition of another and more general nature, namely, that with the other large trading towns of England, and need hardly be told that the greatest part of the necessities of life are advanced considerably in price, beyond that of other towns, the numerous families who have lately settled in

Exeter, and its vicinity, will soon leave it, and seek other residences.

As relates to the new mode, and greater convenience of pursuing this import trade, so dogmatically detailed by the inhabitant of Exeter, that vessels will have first to go to Topsham quay and discharge some of their goods, and then return to Turf to enter the new canal; and again, on coming down the canal, to go upwards again from turf to Topsham, to take in their export goods, the interrogatories he has put are undeserving of notice, and his assertions, though braved out in form so peculiar, must either have been made in complete ignorance of facts, or must have been intended to mislead. The master of any of the vessels accustomed to the river, will inform him that all this passing and re-passing from Topsham to Turf, and back again, twice in one voyage, as so easy and pleasant an operation, is attended with much difficulty and delay, and must depend altogether on the winds and tides.

If, however, it should turn out, which is yet very doubtful, that some vessels may, by entering the new canal at Turf, arrive at Exeter Quay, a few hours, or perhaps a day or two earlier than heretofore, I should conceive that the citizens of Exeter will hardly consider such an insignificant advantage, sufficient to counterbalance all the numerous inconveniences that must now fall on their trade, or an equivalent for the cheap and certain mode pursued by means of the old canal, and I take the liberty, at the present moment, to caution them to contemplate well, all the additional charges they will have to pay for such an accommodation.

AN INHABITANT OF TOPSHAM.

To the Editor of the Exeter Weekly Times,

EXETER CANAL.

SIR – The Exeter Inhabitant having, through the *Flying Post*, imperiously called on that of Topsham to answer certain questions, I beg leave, through your valuable and wide spread journal to make a few observations, though I could have wished your Exeter correspondent had used less invective. As to the chamber having done anything at present to prevent vessels from coming from Turf to Topsham, it is true they have not as yet put a chain across the channel, but they are stopping it in a more gradual and imperceptible way, by diverting Alphington brook, and preventing the ebb and flow of the tide from the old lower sluice to double lock.

The channel from thence, nearly down to the Town of Topsham, is already narrowed one half; and in so short a space time is shallowed 2 feet by the accumulation of sand and mud, owing to the scouring of the tide being lessened, occasioned by Alphington brook with the tide water as heretofore received into the canal from lower sluice to the double locks and let out as usual about low water, being done away. This accumulation, according to Messrs. Whitby & Stuart, who have given their opinion from view (it is supposed as good judges as the chamber or their surveyors), will soon extend itself from one end of the river to the other. A vessel coming in from sea with assorted cargo, some to be landed at Topsham, to be conveyed to Exeter by land carriage, others for the neighbouring districts, first passed the new entrance of the canal at Turf, came up to Topsham which track the said vessel generally can pass through the year 10 days out 14, unloaded the goods destined for Topsham, lightened the vessel say 2 feet, then, if not prevented, passed on its way to Exeter, seldom loosing above 1 day. Arrived at Exeter she discharged the remainder of the cargo and took on board export goods and returned by the same route; finished the cargo at Topsham, and proceeded to her destined port, without travelling one inch out of the usual track.

Now mark what has this vessel to do with the usual annoyance attending the course now dictated by the chamber. She comes in from sea with this assorted cargo, stops at Turf, gets a barge, tumbles over the cargo, rain or shine, puts the goods to be landed at Topsham into luggage craft, which often takes a day or two to accomplish, runs the no small risk of swamping the barge in this exposed open place, sends it to Topsham, where there is a vast deal more work, trouble, and risk of undoing this barge than it would have been in the vessel that brought it, owing to the tackle being insufficient for such purposes and being so much lower. The vessel is at all this trouble and risk rather than go up from Turf to Topsham and back again to the entrance of the new canal, chiefly arising from the probable delay and difficulty of going back to this new entrance. Let it be observed that from Turf to the entrance of the old canal there are 2 shoals, the first beginning just below the town of Topsham, the other from the Passage-house leading up to the usual entrance.

These shoals consist of a mixture of mud and small gravel, very easy for removal: and it has often been surveyed by men who ought to be judges, who say that £5,000 would be sufficient to have deepened the bed of the river 2 feet, and would have answered completely the thing wanted or should it even have cost £10,000, much better than the enormous sum of £100,000 said to be expended. – (Nay what is the large sum collected for town dues, but for removing shoals and sandbanks.) Had this plan been adopted, it would never have come to repair, and no small portion would have been used of the soil so taken up, for ballasting ships, &c.

Again, the Topsham man is accused of selfish and interested views, for re-opening the old entrance. Let me ask, whether the citizens of Exeter would not receive much greater benefit than those of Topsham, if the old right of way was re-established, and goods and merchandize conveyed in small vessels, by their paying the old passing only, than by slumbering and permitting the Chamber to obtain a power to levy what they please! - Let the old Lock be opened again, the usual toll be paid; let these vessels that like, enter the new, the Chamber charge what they think fit. As the Chamber are a body of Trustees for the public, (though they transact their business with closed doors,) if they have nothing but the public interest in view, what is to them whether they take out of the pockets of citizens and others, £7,000 or £10,000 per annum. It ought to be all the same. – Open the old entrance, charge the old dues, and no one will in the least object to, or find fault with the undertaking; the expence will be trifling, and not the least inconvenient.

ANOTHER INHABITANT OF TOPSHAM.

THE CAN OF WORMS? - *Western Times - Saturday 20 January 1838*

EXETER CANAL. Our venerable contemporary, the *Flying Post*, has again opened that deep and vicious wound, the best interests of the city received in the job of all jobs, the extension of the Exeter Canal. The *Flying Post* flings its shafts (as we believe is now pretty well understood) at every person, institution, and principle of a liberal character — but he does it on a bush fighting, and therefore on a cowardly and universally despised system. The columns of his last number bear ample proof of his ultra-tory hatred to all municipal reform, and all persons and parties advocating or upholding it (witness his statements on the Barnstaple, Bath, Totnes, other corporations). But to the question — our contemporary charges that the greatest efforts have been made to abuse the public mind, and set speeches have been made, exhibiting a tolerable share of ignorance on the subject in question. Would our contemporary allow us to ask him, who thus charges others with basely attempting to deceive the public mind, and exhibiting at the same time a gross ignorance of the subject, (two no very consistent accusations be it remembered) whether he is not himself a Councillor, and has not been so since the birth of the New Corporation - whether he has not been present when these speeches, in which he alludes, as displaying such gross ignorance and deception, have been made — and also when the facts and circumstances put forward in these speeches have been printed and circulated among the members of the council — whether he has not again been present, (or ought to have been) on the days appointed for their deliberate consideration and investigation and has he ever designed to say one word, or make one motion, or produce one calculation, return, or document of any kind, by which this deception or ignorance, of which he accuses others, was exposed or detected — and the public, and his brother councillors, protected from them, and enlightened by the superior power of penetrating intellect which God has granted to him, and, according his account, withheld from the ignorant pretenders who have dared (in violation of all tory and *Flying Post* principle) to investigate an unclosed account of public money expended, to the amount of £120,000? We must say that, with Mr. Trewman's strong sense of the *fraud* and *ignorance* attempted, as he alleges, to be practised by some of his brother Councillors upon himself and others of the body, as well as on the public, our Councillor for St. Pauls has, with all his superior knowledge on the subject, done nothing in his capacity of a municipal representative, to protect his constituents from the gross imposition he says has been played off upon them.

But we now, at this very advanced period of the investigation, assure the *Flying Post,* and its Councillor editor, that his article in the last paper proves that he does not, or will not, know what the real complaint or question is — we will tell what it not. It is not whether the Canal ought or not to have been extended; it is not whether the extension was a good or a bad measure; it is not whether trade to this port has been increased or diminished by this extension, it is not whether the city has lost or gained by such extension; it is not whether the income of the Canal has increased since the extension in a greater ratio than it did before. All this it is *not* — and this clearly what the learned editor and Councillor thinks, (or finds it convenient to publish) *it is*. The question really is, whether an extension of one mile and seven furlongs of Canal, with two basins and two locks, estimated by the engineer who executed the work, first at £8,000, then at £11,000, then at £14,000 then at £26,000, and ultimately at £46,000, ought have cost £120,000? and whether that enormous sum ought to have been expended by one or two individual members of the late corporation, in conjunction with the engineer, and the corporation to have been from time to time informed of the excess in the expenditure, *after* it was made, instead of being consulted upon it *before* it was embarked in? and now whether the parties who made such use of their influence, the old corporation, with the most presumptuous confidence in either the ignorance of their brethren, and who aided and abetted the engineer in this monstrous expenditure, cannot and *ought not,* now, to answer to the public, for the whole of the amount which is charged to have been expended upon the work, beyond what it actually has, or with ordinary care and prudence, *ought to have cost.* These are the real questions; and now let us ask the editor of the *Flying Post,* and the Councillor, whether, if the canal now produced a *million* a year, such a circumstance could by any possibility, bear upon these questions. We say no — and we believe no man in his senses can say otherwise.

These, the true questions, should examined and reported upon by competent persons. A resolution of the council was sometime since entered into, for instituting such investigations and if we know anything of the members of the council, whose motives and abilities, it is alike the object of the *Flying Post* to hold to public odium, the article we have alluded to, will have the good effect of making them pursue with renewed energy, an investigation which we fear, might otherwise have been too long deferred, or possibly entirely lost sight of.

With regard to the fact which the *Flying Post* asserts, that the income of the canal is an increasing income, we may say, we have never heard it throughout the whole discussion, denied — how could it be otherwise, with an increasing population, and city, and neighbourhood, equally augmenting in numbers — but what will the *Post* say, if it is proved — as we did in our paper sometime since, by figures — that great as the increase of income has been, if it were doubled or trebled it never will, in the estimation of the most sanguine of the advocates for the extension, pay the interest on the enormous sum charged to have been expended upon it, or give back to the city the revenue it brought to the public purse, when the population of the city and neighbourhood was not so large is now, by many thousand consumers — when the trade was not taxed, in tonnage of vessels passing the works, with more than *one-tenth* the amount they now pay, — but if the income were to overtake the interest on the debt, and to restore the corporation the amount it used to receive, still the work ought to have been executed for £50,000, instead of £120,000, the public interest has been sacrificed to the immense amount of £70,000 besides the enormous sum paid, and to be paid for interest upon this sacrifice.

We know not by what member, or officer of the old or new corporation, the *Flying Post* has been furnished with the figures it published on Thursday, nor do we pretend to say whether ignorance or deception originated this statement, but we will call our readers attention to the manner in which the *Flying Post* proves the trade of the canal increased — he says, the income of 1827, was £4,496, and in 1837, it is £8,651, and the difference he immediately places to the improvement of the canal. Now if this fair-dealing editor did not think proper to assign any part of the augmentation of the revenue, to increased population, and consequently increased capital employed in this city and neighbourhood, there is *one little circumstance* he should, we think, *in his fairness* have stated, and it is this, that by an alteration in the tax or tolls, a vessel of 100 tons, which in 1827, passed the works for 5s, in 1828 (the very next year to that which he *shrewdly* selects to show off his increased income upon) paid the VERY MODERATE ADVANCE of *three pounds fifteen shillings*. The public will, we think, place some considerable part of the increase of income to this unprecedented *extension* of taxation, instead of to this *extension* of the Canal. As Mr. Councillor Trewman, he either did, or did not know this fact; if he did not know it, how shall we rate his ignorance — if he did, what language too strong to describe the deception he has practised in withholding it, whilst he is flinging these foul charges on his brother corporators.

But we are satisfied for the present, with this single instance of our contemporary's fairness, feeling assured that his statement will not be allowed to rest with us, but that he will shortly be afforded a full opportunity in his place as Councillor, of convicting those members of his body, if he can, of the very charges — from which, we think, it will require even all his talents to defend himself with success.

Appendix 8

The Commissioners' Report Exeter 1834

"**The Corporations of England and Wales**": (collected and abridged from The Reports of the Commissioners for enquiring into Municipal Corporations) by A.E. (Alexander James Edmund) Cockburn, Esq. Barrister-at-Law (one of the Commissioners) Vol I (in two volumes), 1835, p.32-38.

DEVON – CITY OF EXETER. – Population, 28,242.

The city claims to be a Corporation by prescription: The Governing Charter is the one of *3 Charles I*. The City is a distinct County of itself.

The CORPORATION consists of a Mayor, eight Alderman, twenty-four Common Councilmen (including the Mayor and the Aldermen), and an indefinite body of Freemen.

The GOVERNING BODY is composed of the twenty-four just mentioned, who form the Common Council, or, as it is called, the Chamber of the City. They have the authority to make bye-laws for the regulation of the city: two only, while relate to the Market, are now in operation.

The Debt of the Corporation amounts to £141,309. Mortgages have been given for £44,900; bonds for £9,647; canal specific bonds for £78,600. In the bond debt is included a sum of £2,000 to Sir Thomas Acland, for the balance of Church Stowe charity; among the mortgages a debt to Lord Rolle of £14,000. Of the debt £107,327 were expended on the canal, £35,000 on the market. The charity commissioners found that the corporation were indebted to the various charities £67,280. It has been agreed that this sum should be paid by annual instalments. Other Suits have been brought against them in respect of Charities of which they are trustees, and they have been obliged to pay into court £86,541. The accounts of the corporation are regularly kept and audited. They are the Trustees of extensive Charities.

The Corporation of Exeter, being self-elected, and conducting their affairs in private meeting, have not gained the confidence of the inhabitants. It is true there has been no appropriation of the funds of the Corporation to the purposes of individual members of the body, nor has there been any partiality or unfairness in the letting or selling of their lands and houses, the Members of the Corporate body and the other inhabitants being precisely on the same footing in these respects. But the Corporation have not administered the public property with prudence or discretion, whilst their misappropriation to corporate purposes of the funds for which they were Trustees for Charities, subjects them to serious reproach. With an ample income for public purposes, under an economical but liberal expenditure, sufficient for all of the objects of a municipal government, they have been constantly increasing the Corporate Debt. The Expenditure on the Canal has been most improvident; a debt of more than £100,000 has been incurred on this account alone. Not only on ground of having undertaken a work, the advantages attending which never were likely to be at all equal to the outlay, is the prudence of the corporation to be questioned, but the plan which they adopted in carrying that work into execution cannot be too strongly condemned. With an estimate amounting to less than half the actual expenditure, without public contracts, and therefore without competition, this enormous cost cannot have been under proper control.

The Works at the Canal were not constructed by public contract, and the enormous expenditure on the improvement of the canal was the subject of much complaint on the part of some of the merchants of the City. It appears that the Corporation, when they embarked in this work at first, only contemplated repairing the old Canal; but they afterwards resolved on considerably extending the work. On the old Canal the passage of vessels was frequently delayed for want of water, and no vessel drawing more than nine feet could conveniently approach the city. The Canal has doubtless materially increased the facility of vessels reaching the city, and it has enabled vessels of a greater draught to enter the Port at dead neap tides. In consequence of this alteration, the tolls have been materially increased upon many articles, and the charges bear a large proportion to the freight; sometimes as much as a fourth part of the freight on a coasting voyage. Whatever difference of opinion may exist as to the expediency of the alteration, there can be but one opinion as to the manner in which the work has been carried to execution. In the year 1819, an engineer was desired to survey the works for the purpose of repairing and improving them; and in consequence of a report then made by him, considerable alterations were made, and the locks, gates, &c. were put into complete repair. In 1824, the engineer made a further report, and recommended, for various reasons, the extension of the Canal to a place called Turf one mile seven furlongs lower down the River than the Lower Sluices of the then existing Canal. This report was submitted to Mr. Telford, and was confirmed by him. In May, 1825, the work was commenced; but it does not appear that the Corporation had either estimate or contract for the work done in 1824; nor was any estimate given for the work commenced in 1825, until the following year, when a further Report, with an estimate for completing the canal, with the bridge and basin, amounting to £45,391, was delivered. In the year 1831, it was stated that the further sum of £10,921 would be requisite to complete the canal without the bridge. This sum was supplied, and the corporation, without obtaining a further estimate, and without the precaution of having the work executed by public contracts, proceeded to supply the further funds demanded from them for this work, until they had expended on the works alone £95,000, together with land purchased for the quay, £5,400, and the incidental charges, £5,627, amounting in all to £106,527. Under the new Act for making these alterations, the tolls have been much increased. The old canal, at the lower tolls, yielded a revenue of rather more than £4,000 per annum. Before the late Act, vessels passing the canal paid a duty of 5s.6d. each, without reference to the burthen. Under the new Act, the corporation are empowered to levy 5s. on all vessels using the canal locks or basins under ten tons burthen; 6d. per ton on all vessels above ten tons and under 100 tons; and on all above 110 tons, 9d. per ton.

The neglect of the Quay at Topsham, and the suffering the River to be gradually choking up, are also matters of well-founded complaint against the body. The inhabitants of the latter place complain that the corporation of Exeter take Quay Dues at Topsham, and that they have not only not kept the Quay at that place in good repair, but that the inhabitants, who have been obliged to erect wharfs and quays in consequence of the neglect of the corporation in this respect, are notwithstanding compelled to pay quay dues to the corporation, though they do not use the corporation quay. The corporation have it in contemplation to erect a new crane and to repair the quay. Serious complaints are also made of the negligence of the corporation respecting the river. In all cases where the right to the Town Dues has been questioned, the corporation are stated to have alleged the cleansing of the harbour as a consideration. At present they certainly neglect to perform this important duty – a duty rendered much more serious, both with regard to the necessity as well as to the expense of its performance, since the new Canal has been constructed. It was stated by pilots, and other competent persons, that before the new canal was constructed, vessels drawing thirteen feet water could be brought alongside the quay at Topsham at spring tides, and vessels drawing ten feet at neap tides. The tides in the Exe are much affected by the wind, the extreme difference between spring and neap tides varying from five feet to seven feet. At the lowest neap tides, vessels drawing ten feet cold formerly be taken over the shoals; this could be done seven or eight years ago; but within the last eight years, the depth of water at Topsham has decreased a foot and a half. Two years since, the steam vessel *The William the Fourth*, drawing ten and a half feet to eleven feet, could be brought to the wharf just below Topsham Quay: but this cannot now be done, by reason of the water having decreased a foot and a half. The channel is filling up, both in the sides and the centre. Since the embankment for the canal, which has enclosed a great space over which the tide formerly flowed, there is not nearly the same quantity of backwater; and probably some part of the evil has been occasioned by the confining of the water in the canal, which used to be let out by the lower sluice; the current was strong, and contributed to keep the channel clear. The bottom of the river is mud and gravel, which might be removed by the dredging. The attention of the corporation has been called to the state of the river, In December, 1832, an application was made to the corporation respecting the choking of the channel, which application was not answered until May, 1833, when it was said it would be taken into consideration. The proprietors of steam-boats trading between Topsham and London have expressed their willingness to meet the corporation in the way of contribution of cleansing the harbour. It may be conceived that the owners of the vessels have a great interest in preserving the passage to the quay, when it is known that the expense of voyage of a steam-boat, when she cannot approach the quay, is £8 greater than when she lands her cargo at the quay. If something be not speedily done, the trade of Topsham will be very seriously injured; and the corporation will exact dues for quays which shipping cannot approach, and towns dues in consideration of cleansing a port, one part of which is fast choking up. The engineer who constructed the canal, denied that the embankment had anything to do with the obstructions in the navigation.

Judging from the evidence tendered by several persons interested in the trade of Exeter, it appears that the payment of the Town Dues is felt to be a severe tax upon the non-freemen, and certainly the inhabitants of Topsham have much reason to complain, if not of the collection of the dues, yet of the neglect of the performance of those services which the corporation have frequently assigned as a reason for exacting them. It must, however, be admitted, that in the present state of the corporate property, the members of the body have the power of doing very little. The income is almost entirely absorbed by the payment of the interest of the debt, and the current expenses. For the misappropriation of charity funds, the recent members of the corporation are not accountable, and at this time the management of the charities appears to be very excellent; the impropriety of contracting a vast share of the overwhelming debt of the Corporation belongs to the present body.

The inhabitants assessed to the relief of the poor have cause of complaint, arising from the conduct of the corporation in respect to Atwill's and the Awilscombe Charities. The Corporation of the Poor, finding that the funds of these charities, which, under the will of the donors, ought to be given to the poor, had been, in their opinion, misapplied, instituted two Chancery suits respecting them. The Corporation, however, appealed against the application of the poor-rate to the purpose of carrying on these suits; and the City Sessions, where Members of the Corporate Body are the only judges, decided that the Corporation of the Poor ought not to apply the funds. The suits have not, in consequence, been pressed with rigour.

The Commissioners

Buoy Number 36 (Red) - Port Lateral -
50°41.272'N 003°28.514' W – FL.R.5s

The Port of Topsham River Commissioners

James Norton, Mark Mills, Eliot Wright, Godfrey Whitehouse
Their Clerk – Thomas Epton

Harbourmaster for the Port of Exeter

Mr Grahame Forshaw, MBE, MNI

Playbill for "The First Cut - or Isabella's Revenge", written by Alan Caig, esq.

References and Citations

The following first two published works are key texts for any study of the Port and the River Exe and Canal and full acknowledgement and all references are given accordingly, as well as to all the other Books and Resources listed.

Clark, E. A. G., *The Ports of the Exe Estuary, 1660-1860 - A Study in Historical Geography*," University of Exeter, 1960

Clew, Kenneth R., *The Exeter Canal*, Phillimore, 1984.

Topsham Museum, *Topsham & Sugar*, Topsham Museum Research Project, 2021.

Hoskins, W. G., *Industry, Trade and People in Exeter, 1688-1800*, Manchester University Press, 1935

Williams, Eric, *Capitalism and Slavery*, The University of North Carolina Press, 1944.

MacCaffrey, Wallace T., *Exeter, 1540–1640*, 1975, Harvard University Press

Newton, Robert, *Eighteenth Century Exeter*, University of Exeter, 1984

De la Garde, Philip Chilwell, *Memoir of the Canal of Exeter, from 1563 to 1724*, Proceedings of the Institution of Civil Engineers, Vol. IV., 1845. (ed. Charles Manby)

Green, James, M. Inst. C. E., *Memoir of the Canal of Exeter, continuation from 1819 to 1830*, Proceedings of the Institution of Civil Engineers, Vol. IV., 1845. (ed. Charles Manby)

Pugsley, David, *Follett Our Great Lawyer*, Doderidge Club, Law Faculty, University of Exeter, 1991

George, Brian. *James Green - Canal Builder and County Surveyor (1781 - 1849)*, Devon Books, 1997.

Other Sources

The Devon Heritage Centre, Exeter

Topsham Museum – **Research and Archival Records and Support**

Newspaper Reports – *The Western Times, The Exeter Flying Post, The Exeter & Plymouth Gazette*

Messrs. Ashfords (solicitors) - **Extracts from a Report to Exeter City Council**, in respect of the proposals for a Harbour Revision Order, as prepared by M/s Lara Moore (Head of the Ports and Harbours and Transport Division) and her Team, 2022.

"From troubles of the world I turn to Ducks."
F.W. Harvey - 1919

The Introduction	"Ibsen"
Chapter One	" Benvenuto Cellini"
Chapter Two	"Orwell"
Chapter Three	"Jonathan Livingston Seagull"
Chapter Four	"Nina's Duck"
Chapter Five	"Prufrock"
Chapter Six	"John Naughton"
Chapter Seven	"Dea's Duck"
Chapter Eight	"Jill's Shorebird"
Chapter Nine	"Horace" *(Quintus Horatius Flaccus)*
Chapter Ten	"Edward Andrea-Jones"
Chapter Eleven	"Cigar Daisy"
Chapter Twelve	"Daphne's Duck"
Chapter Thirteen	"Chekhov"
Chapter Fourteen	"Spud"
Chapter Fifteen	" Ibsen" (Revisited)
Afterword	"The Perfect Egg – an Attempt"
	(...Try again, Fail again, Fail Better...)

"...All God's jokes are good – even the practical ones! And as for the duck, I think God must have smiled a bit... on the day He fashioned it..."

F.W. Harvey - 1919

Tom Epton, from the West Riding of Yorkshire, now lives in White Street, Topsham. Educated at a Methodist School in Suffolk, and an Alumnus of Christ's College, Cambridge, he was a Provincial Solicitor for four decades and a one-time Decoy Duck Carver.

He has given service to Community interests and Offices wherever living, contributing Pieces and Reviews to local Journals and, of late, delivering Eulogies for good Friends who have crossed the river.

His Membership of Topsham Sailing Club is integral to his love of Sailing & the Waters of the Exe.

The "Work in Progress" (be it of Painting or of Father) is with the kind permission of Nina Epton